The Guide to
Kimono

The Guide to
Kimono

A HANDBOOK TO IDENTIFYING, DATING, AND PRICING ANTIQUE AND VINTAGE JAPANESE KIMONO

SCHIFFER
PUBLISHING

4880 Lower Valley Road • Atglen, PA 19310

Justine Sobocan

Contents

Preface

Since Japan opened its ports to the West in 1854, the kimono has been one of the most recognizable symbols of the country. No other type of clothing is better known or more mysterious to outsiders than the kimono; its allure has fascinated the world over, yet most kimono knowledge has never been translated from its native Japanese or published outside Japan. Some of this knowledge can be found online, but it is not always accessible to the general public and is almost always written in Japanese.

Learning about kimono over the past decade has become akin to learning a trade; you can only truly learn from people who are established in the field, and you need to repeatedly see and feel the product to know what you're dealing with. At first kimono may seem the same, but with time you can distinguish them by touch, or by the most minute color differences, or with the motifs that make them wearable works of art. Although this book will not make you a master overnight, it will definitely clear up the confusion about the terms, motifs, and basic information that surround kimono. A quick internet search will lead you to millions of pages of false information. Unless you know the specific terms for what you're researching, this can be daunting to people who are curious about kimono but don't know where to start.

I was prompted to write this book after seeing so many people who list kimono for sale online but have no idea what they really have. It was especially disheartening when so-called professional appraisers for various auction houses and appraisal services consistently identified either the product or the value incorrectly. There are small groups of people in the Western world who study and collect kimono, but since there is no official capacity in which to be a specialist outside Japan, getting true information to a wider audience is very hard to do. This is the aim of this book: to dispel some of the confusion about kimono from the Western consciousness.

A final note: Japanese words are both singular and plural. So when speaking about multiple examples of this garment, you would not say "kimonos" but simply "kimono." Also, all *kana*, or Japanese letter pairings, are pronounced, so a word such as *tomesode* would be pronounced "to-mé-so-dé" and not "tohm-sohd."

Introduction

What Is (and Isn't) a Kimono?

The term **kimono** (着物), which means "thing to wear," originally encompassed any type of clothing in Japan. Once the West saw these magnificent garments, the word quickly became used for the specific item we now call the kimono; all other types of clothing were given a different term: **wafuku** (和服). Translated as "native dress," wafuku encompasses any clothing native to Japan, including kimono, when speaking in general terms or of collections of different types of Japanese clothing. The act of putting on and wearing kimono is known as **kitsuke** (着付け). The kimono as we know it developed during the Heian period (794–1185). It was during this time that nobility began wearing a T-shaped garment with rectangular sleeves in layers. These magnificent outfits were often worn in twelve layers, known as **junihitoe** (十二単), which were carefully color-coordinated to match the current season. The kimono would slowly morph into the garment that we know today over the next few centuries, being nearly indistinguishable from modern examples by the dawn of the Edo period (1603–1868).

A kimono is a garment made of carefully measured fabric panels that are sewn together in such a way that the garment can fit almost anyone and has a pattern that is best viewed when worn. It is put on using a prescribed set of steps unique to the garment that are now often taught by special *kitsuke* schools, since the act of wearing kimono on a daily basis has mostly been lost from the Japanese consciousness. Nowadays, kimono are worn only to special events, such as weddings, or by professional artists, such as dancers.

Over time, cheap imitations have taken over the Western view of what a kimono is. The vast majority of these export kimono do not subscribe to the rules described above but, rather, focus on how easily a person can put the garment on. A traditional kimono cannot just be put on; a person must follow certain steps to wear it correctly. However, many Western buyers want the look of a kimono but not the difficulty, thus leading to the large quantities of export kimono that are not even kimono at all.

Here are some tips for inspecting a garment that you have been told is a kimono but that you suspect is an export item.

Thin, shiny fabric: Most export kimono are made from a synthetic fabric that has a satin look and feel. No real kimono are made from this type of fabric, since kimono are not meant to be mass-produced.

Tags: It is extremely rare to find a tag on a real kimono. If present, they are located on the inside panel, closest to the collar, on the left-hand side; they will contain information about the store that sold it and will always be written in Japanese. If you find a tag stitched on the collar, especially one that says "Made in Japan," you are dealing with an export kimono.

Matching belt and belt loops: If there are loops for a belt attached to the main garment, you are dealing with an export kimono. Most export kimono have a piece of fabric used for a belt to keep the garment closed; it will be made from the same fabric with the same pattern as the garment. Some belts have a bow on top of a box-shaped part that is meant to be worn on the waist for decoration. Real kimono never have belts or belt loops.

Heavy embroidery: To make their products more alluring, export kimono companies will add heavily embroidered symbols, such as dragons, that are rarely found on real kimono. They will also use embroidery only to apply the motifs, unlike real kimono, which have motifs made from a combination of embroidery and hand painting or dyeing.

If your garment doesn't have any of these giveaways, congratulations!
You are likely the owner of a real kimono. Keep reading to
find out more about your garment.

An example of an export
kimono. Notice the shiny,
thin material.

Part I

Chapter 1

Male, Female, and Formality

Whether made for a man or a woman, a kimono is still called a kimono. The layout of the panels is the same, but there is one major difference: the sleeves.

When it comes to men's kimono, the sleeves have openings only at the front, to allow for hands to pass through. Women's kimono have additional openings at the back of the sleeves called *miyatsuguchi* (身八つ口) that help the wearer put on the garment properly and make her movements look more elegant. Children's kimono will always have both sides of the sleeves open to help dress them.

Another noticeable difference is the decoration. Men's kimono tend to be plain, with decoration only on the inside lining. Women's kimono can be either quite simple or covered with luxurious painted motifs or embroidery.

A male kimono without miyatsuguchi (*top*) and a female kimono with miyatsuguchi (*bottom*)

One important decoration that can be found on the most formal kimono of both men and women is **kamon** (家紋). Translated as "family symbol," these icons are about the size of a quarter for women and a golf ball for men. In the earlier part of the twentieth century, kamon were common on formal kimono since they are a physical representation of a family and its wealth. If you could purchase or commission a luxurious kimono with kamon, you would wear it to the most important social gatherings, where people would recognize you as belonging to a specific family, even if they didn't know who you were.

An assortment of kamon

Kamon are a way of literally wearing your wealth on your sleeves. The number of kamon on a kimono—whether one, three, or five—also denotes its formality. Although uncommon on contemporary examples, they are a valuable resource for estimating a kimono's age. Here is an explanation of kamon and their placement on the garment as an indicator of formality.

1 Found on the back of the kimono, just under the collar, a single kamon meant that a kimono was formal but could still be worn to casual social gatherings. This usage fell out of fashion after World War II.

3 In addition to the placement of the single kamon, an additional two may be found on the back of each sleeve. These remained rare after World War II but were used into the 1960s before disappearing after that date.

5 Along with the previous three, two more may be added to the back, near the top of the sleeves. Having five kamon symbolizes the highest formality, and these kimono would be worn only on very special occasions. Their use largely fell out of fashion around the same time as three kamon. However, they are still used today on the most formal black kimono worn at weddings by the mothers of the bride and groom.

Chapter 2
Types of Kimono

Kimono are assigned specific terms, depending on the location of motifs or the type of fabric used to make them. When researching kimono, it is always best to use these words, not just the word "kimono," which is too vague. Otherwise, you'll be left sorting through tens of thousands of items to find something comparable to what you have. The majority of these terms apply to women's kimono.

Because there isn't really any type for the male version of the garment, these are simply called **men's kimono** (男の着物). Their fabrics are often plain, solid colors and devoid of decoration. You can tell men's kimono from women's by the lack of miyatsuguchi.

A Late Showa–period men's kimono
$50–$75

Unlike an adult kimono, which will last a lifetime, a *child's kimono* will be worn only a handful of times. One use takes place during their first visit to a shrine after their birth, called **omiyamairi** (お宮参り), which is akin to a Christian baptism. Other uses of the garment occur on **shichigosan** (七五三), the day in November when children visit their local shrine to pray to the gods for good health in the future. Shichigosan literally means "7-5-3," which are the ages when the children will visit. Boys will go to the shrine in their third and fifth years, and girls will go in the third and seventh years, with many children going at all three ages for extra protection. The children are blessed by a priest and given sacred arrows to ward off danger. Girls will wear a small *furisode* known as a **mitsumi** (三つ身), and boys will wear a *haori* with *hakama* (see chapters 5 and 6). The defining feature that allows you to tell them apart from other kimono is that they'll have wide silk bands sewn into the front to allow for easy dressing.

A purple Taisho-period girl's mitsumi with
chrysanthemums
$100–$150

ANATOMY OF A KIMONO

eri (襟/衿): The collar of a kimono (See chapter 4 for more information.)
sode (袖): Sleeves that are rectangular in shape. The opening at the front of the sleeves is called **sodeguchi** (袖口), and the opening at the back of the sleeves is called **miyatsuguchi** (身八つ口).
haba (幅): The width of a panel of kimono fabric
senui (背縫い): The middle seam that divides the kimono in half
susosen (裾先): The hemline of a kimono

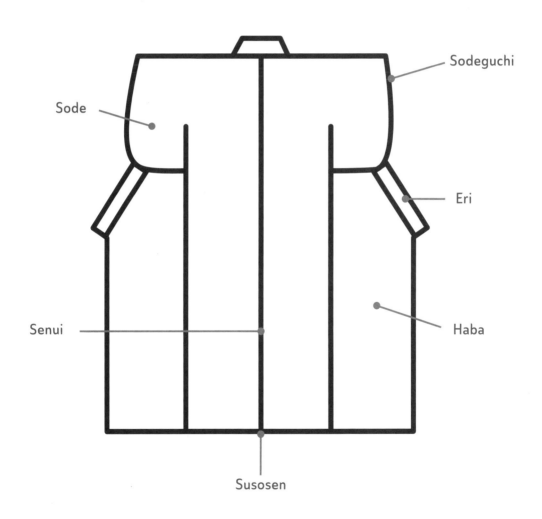

KOSODE (小袖): "Short Sleeves"

Any kimono with sleeves that do not extend past the waist is known as kosode. Short sleeves can be found on both formal and informal kimono, and the term applies to both men's and women's examples. The vast majority of kimono have the short sleeves of a kosode, so it is a vague term that should not often be used.

A Late Showa–period komon with kosode sleeves
$50

FURISODE (振袖): "Swinging Sleeves"

This type of kimono with long sleeves is worn only by unmarried women. The sleeves are meant to flutter and attract the attention of a potential suitor. A furisode can be both formal and informal, depending on its decoration, sleeve length, and presence of crests. Today, furisode can range anywhere in formality from everyday wear to the most formal of dress, depending on the sleeves.

It was a common practice before World War II to cut the sleeves of a bride's furisode so that she could continue to wear the kimono as a married woman. Since these kimono always had five crests, they were highly formal and would then take the name of *tomesode* or *houmongi*, depending on the position of motifs.

Furisode sleeves come in
three different lengths:

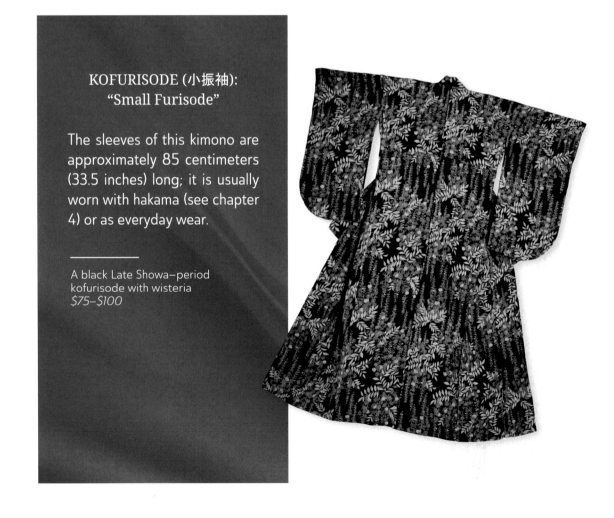

KOFURISODE (小振袖): "Small Furisode"

The sleeves of this kimono are approximately 85 centimeters (33.5 inches) long; it is usually worn with hakama (see chapter 4) or as everyday wear.

A black Late Showa–period kofurisode with wisteria
$75–$100

CHŪFURISODE (中振袖)
"Middle Furisode"

The sleeves of this kimono are 100 centimeters (39 inches) in length and can be of almost any level of formality.

A bright-red Late Showa–period chūfurisode with wisteria
$100–$150

ŌFURISODE (大振袖)
"Large Furisode"

Sleeves are 120 centimeters (47 inches), now the most common size for sleeves. They are used for the furisode of the highest formality.

A white Early Showa–period ōfurisode with paulownia and shibori
$200–$250

Types of Kimono

UCHIKAKE (打掛): "Dragging Outer Garment"

This very special type of kimono is worn by a bride only on her wedding. Before the nineteenth century, uchikake were also used by nobility, but they were not as heavy or as elaborate as modern uchikake and fell out of fashion around the turn of the twentieth century. From the early 1900s to the Second World War, uchikake were considered too old-fashioned by brides, but they lived on as stage costumes; their rich decoration of elaborate embroidery was meant to be seen from far away. The old courtesans, who are often depicted as heroes in kabuki plays, used to wear uchikake because it was a symbol of their wealth and popularity. Once Japan began to westernize in the 1950s and 1960s, uchikake reemerged and became popular for brides and their families. Many people wanted to wear kimono again, and thus began a revival for the most formal (and expensive) types of kimono.

Along with the traditional uchikake, which are very colorful and full of lucky motifs, there now exists a completely white uchikake, known as a *shiromuku* (白無垢), which is meant to imitate the traditional white dress of a Western bride. Because of their elaborately embroidered patterns and heavy weight, uchikake tend to be rented out more often than bought, since the cost would be about as much as the wedding itself. All new or vintage uchikake will be furisode, whereas antique ones can be furisode or kosode.

A black Meiji-period uchikake with
phoenixes and paulownia
$1,500–$2,000

TOMESODE (留袖): "Fastened Sleeves"

This is the most formal type of kimono worn by married women. "Fastened" refers to the long sleeves of a furisode that were traditionally cut when a woman married. The defining feature of a tomesode is that its decoration is found only below the waist. **Iro** (色), or "colored," tomesode were common before World War II, but now almost all new tomesode are **kuro** (黒), or "black," tomesode.

A blue Taisho-period irotomesode
with boats
$100–$150

A Late Showa–period kurotomesode
with birds and waves
$50

HOUMONGI (訪問着): "Visiting Wear"

This is the second most formal type of kimono worn by married women. Decoration can be found all over its exterior and will flow in one continuous scene along the entire piece. Many formal houmongi will resemble tomesode, but if you find decoration on the sleeves or shoulders, then you're dealing with a houmongi.

A purple Late Showa–period
houmongi with waves
$75–$100

TSUKESAGE (付け下げ): "Attached Downward"

The midlevel in kimono formality. This term comes from a broken pattern that does not connect across the garment but instead stays only within its own panel and points upward in a vertical formation. Tsukesage can be worn to everyday places, such as restaurants, or even to weddings, but only if the wearer is not a member of the immediate family of the bride or groom. Tsukesage and houmongi are often confused with each other since they can look quite similar, so always check the flow and positioning of the overall pattern to determine which one you have.

A black Late Showa–period tsukesage
with irises showing off its signature
vertical formation
$75–$100

IROMUJI (色無地): "Single Plain Color"

A kimono that is devoid of any decoration and consists of just a solid-colored fabric. Many iromuji have crests, especially on men's kimono, and can then be worn to formal events. Without the crests, the iromuji becomes something that can be worn as an everyday kimono. Formal iromuji tend to have beautiful patterns woven into the silk itself, while plain iromuji, made either from silk or rayon, will just have a simple, soft feel to them.

A purple Late Showa–period iromuji
with a single kamon
$50

KOMON (小紋): "Small Pattern"

An informal type of kimono that is meant to be worn as everyday wear. It is characterized by patterns, either woven, embroidered, or dyed, that are repeated throughout the garment. These make up the majority of casual or informal kimono and come in a vast array of colors and styles.

A multicolored Late Showa–period
komon with maple leaves and branches
$50

YUKATA (浴衣): "Bathrobe"

A cotton kimono worn only during the summer months. The term originally came about because these very casual and easy-to-put-on kimono are meant to be worn when entering and exiting a bath at a hot spring. A yukata is completely informal and suitable to wear only to casual outdoor activities, such as festivals or sightseeing. The light cotton allows the wearer to keep cool during the summer heat, and the patterns follow the same rules as a komon. Some new yukata are made of synthetic fibers that make them easier to wash, but a yukata will never be made of silk. Yukata are also worn by men.

A blue Heisei-period yukata
with morning glories
$50

Lined versus Unlined

The majority of kimono are *awase* (袷), which means that there's an inner lining to complete the garment and keep the wearer warm. This inner lining, which is often patterned on the hem of older kimono, is called a *hakkake* (八掛). A kimono without a lining, seen mostly in summer kimono, is known as *hitoe* (単衣).

An awase kimono (*left*) and a hitoe kimono (*right*)

Exceptions to the Rule

About 95 percent of kimono will fall into the above categories, but there are a few kimono types that are a subtype of a subtype, which significantly affect value.

KARINUI (仮縫い): "Temporary Stitching"

A kimono of any type whose stitching has been only loosely done to show the finished shape of the garment. These pieces will require a lining (if applicable) and final stitching by someone who is well versed in sewing kimono. Due to the work involved in completing a kimono and the inability to be worn, karinui are often cheap, unless they are handmade by a skilled artisan and have yet to be completed since the painting or decorating was finished.

HIKIZURI (引き摺り): "Trailing Garment" or
SUSOHIKI (裾引き): "Trailing Skirt"

Made as both kosode and furisode, these kimono are much longer than a normal kimono since they have an extended skirt that is meant to trail on the ground when worn. The terms refer to the same kimono but differ depending on what region of Japan you live in. Southern places such as Osaka (with the exception of Kyoto) will call them *susohiki*, whereas northern places, such as Tokyo, will call them *hikizuri*. Each term is correct to use with this type of kimono, but hikizuri tends to be a bit more popular than susohiki when it comes to searches and archives. For hundreds of years the majority of kimono were worn trailing on the ground, since the length of a kimono was a symbol of wealth. By the late nineteenth century, trailing kimono were falling out of fashion with Japan's wealthiest citizens and survived through to the present day only due to one specific group of people: dancers.

Elaborate costumes worn on a kabuki stage or by a **geisha** (芸者—literally "person of art / artist") in her daily work are the only modern examples of hikizuri/susohiki still being made. Although they are rare today, there are many vintage and antique hikizuri/susohiki floating around the market due to Japan's economic boom before World War II. It is estimated that there were approximately 80,000 geisha who worked all over the country, and the most popular ones had closets full of hikizuri/susohiki. As with the dialect differences between hikizuri and susohiki, you will often see geisha called *geiko* (芸妓—literally "woman of art") in southern Japan.

A blue Early Showa–period geisha hikizuri/susohiki with summer lilies
$500–$750

A hikizuri/susohiki can be identified through the following characteristics:

Length: Newer hikizuri/susohiki are around 190 centimeters (75 inches) or longer, while antique ones can be as short as 160 centimeters (63 inches). The length of the skirt, measured from just under the end of the collar, should make up approximately 55 to 60 percent of the entire length of the garment.

Pattern: The pattern of a hikizuri/susohiki will always go above the bottom of the collar on the skirt of the kimono. Examples meant for stage use often have padding at the end of the skirts or an extra skirt sewn on to prevent the outer one from becoming dirty while it is being dragged along the ground. The extra skirt is called a *hiyoku* (比翼), which translates as "second wing" since it often flutters when worn. Many formal, non-hikizuri/susohiki kimono will also have hiyoku for this same reason.

Motifs: Unlike changing fashion trends, the motifs on hikizuri/susohiki are mostly static and display only traditional motifs such as native flowers and lucky symbols. Western motifs are extremely rare and can be found only on newer hikizuri/susohiki that are used in stage performances.

Material: All older and elaborate hikizuri/susohiki are made of silk. Some newer examples for stage use are made of synthetic fibers, such as polyester, so they can be washed, but the majority continue to be made from silk.

KAKESHITA (掛下): "Hanging Down"

A trailing furisode worn under an uchikake at a wedding. They technically fit the definition as a type of hikizuri/susohiki since the skirt is meant to trail on the ground, but, like an uchikake, they are meant to be worn only once. Kakeshita designs are heavily influenced by current fashion trends and tend to have an abundance of lucky symbols associated with marriage and a large palette of bold colors. A kakeshita can also have a hiyoku attached to it, but it is almost always red, since red is considered a very lucky and auspicious color.

Despite being closely related to hikizuri/susohiki, those terms should never be used for a kakeshita. Kakeshita are meant for weddings, while hikizuri/susohiki are for performances by skilled artists.

HAGOROMO (羽衣): "Feather Robe"

A new and popular trend for brides that was originally conceived for use on stage, this thin, transparent furisode is worn like an uchikake on top of the outfit to give the wearer an air of divinity. The name comes from the story of the Hagoromo, a robe of feathers that allowed gods to fly. They are sometimes found under the name of *ōganji wasō* (オーガンジー和装), which translates as "organza Japanese-style clothing."

A pink Late Showa–period kakeshita
with orchids
$150–$200

EDO KOMON (江戸小紋): "Edo-Style Komon"

A type of kimono that's a mix between a komon and an iromuji. It's made up of very fine patterns in a single color, giving it the look of an iromuji from far away but a komon up close. Because of its similarities, it is on par with an iromuji when it comes to formality.

A pink Late Showa–period
Edo komon
$50–$75

MOFUKU (喪服): "Mourning Wear"

Solid black kimono, obi, and accessories that are worn to funerals. Showing patterns or decorations at such an event is considered disrespectful to the deceased, but recently some DIY kimono designers use mofuku kimono and obi as a base to paint their own designs, since they are quite cheap to acquire.

A Late Showa–period
mofuku featuring five kamon
$50

Chapter 3
Materials and Techniques

Kimono are as varied as fingerprints, making the materials and techniques that go into their production as important as the garment itself. Being able to identify them is paramount to understanding them. When combined, they are the factors that ultimately determine value, so pay close attention to the following.

MATERIALS

Most kimono tend to be made from silk, but there are myriad new fabrics coming into the marketplace that are much easier to care for and can produce a similar product at a fraction of the cost. This is not to say that silk isn't worth the price—it just means that more options than ever before are available for the kimono connoisseur. Knowing what your kimono is made of is incredibly important, since this information will have the largest percentage of value assigned to it.

Animal-Based Fabrics

Kinu/silk (絹): Used in the overwhelming majority of older kimono and many pieces made today. It is both lightweight and strong, so it's perfect for clothing.

Ro (絽): A special type of silk weave used in summer garments. It's meant to keep the wearer cool and allow for more air to circulate around the body. It looks like horizontal lines when present on a kimono.

Sha (紗): A sheer, almost transparent type of silk used in summer garments. It is also known as "gauze silk" by English speakers.

Shusu (繻子): A thick, satin silk that was used for formal uchikake and obi during the Meiji and Taisho periods. Its robust strength allowed for heavy embroidery to stay firmly anchored and produced a shine that would make the wearer the center of attention. It fell out of fashion during the Late Taisho period, when painterly designs replaced heavy embroidery as the most stylish kimono technique.

Shioze (塩瀬): Thick silk with a clear weft pattern that is often used for items that will endure much folding and bending, such as obi or eri.

Chirimen (ちりめん): A type of silk crepe that is more durable and textured than traditional silk. However, it can be a bit heavier than normal silk, so it is best used in kimono made for cold weather.

Kinsha (金紗): A thin type of chirimen that is commonly found on summer kimono

Yomo/wool (羊毛): A much more recent addition to the list of fabrics, wool is used mostly for informal kimono such as yukata or komon.

Synthetic Fabrics

Jinken/rayon (人絹: **"man-made silk"**): One of the first synthetic fibers used in Japanese clothing. Rayon can be washed and stored much easier than silk. It can also hold certain colors of dyes better than silk, but the difference can be very hard to make out. Some prewar pieces can be found, but rayon kimono became much more common in the 1950s and 1960s. Unlike most synthetic fibers, rayon is plant based, since it is made from wood pulp.

Polyester (ポリエステル): A popular fabric in new, nonformal kimono. Unlike silk, it is easy to wash and take care of, so it's perfect for people who are new to kimono. A majority of new juban are made out of polyester, since it is common to perspire while wearing a kimono, and having the ability to wash and freshen your juban yourself makes wearing a kimono much easier.

Plant-Based Fabrics

Wata/cotton (綿): Used solely for yukata and other very informal wear, it is light and cheap and keeps a person cool in the summer heat. A popular type of cotton weave for older fabrics is muslin.

Asa/hemp (麻): This plant-based fabric was used mostly for the clothing of peasants and farmers since it was much cheaper to produce than silk. However, in the Edo period, hemp was just as fashionable as silk for formal kimono. Hemp is a very light and soft fabric, but it does not have the same durability as silk, so you will rarely ever see this in contemporary pieces.

Jofu/ramie (上布): A plant in the flax family that has incredibly strong and durable fibers. It is, however, quite coarse, so it is usually blended with hemp to make it more comfortable to wear. Since both ramie and hemp produce very light weaves, their fabrics are almost always exclusively found in summer outfits.

Determining Materials: The Burn Test

One of the easiest ways to test what kind of material your fabric is made out of is called the burn test, which involves the removal of a single thread (or even a small piece of fabric) and lighting it on fire, either with a lighter or small tea light (a strong flame is not recommended!). If you are going to perform this test, then please be sure to hold the thread with a pair of tweezers or another tool that is not connected to your skin. Additionally, the test should always be performed in a well-ventilated area. When the thread is lit, you need to compare the look and smell for identification purposes. The three main materials groups are these:

1. **Protein (animal-based):** Burns slowly and will try to "wiggle" away from the flame. Not much smoke is produced, but it does smell like burning hair and has brittle ashes that will crumble if you touch them.

2. **Cellulose (plant-based):** Burns very quickly, with white or light-gray smoke and light-gray ash that is very soft. It can continue to smolder after the flame has been extinguished, and it smells like burnt paper or leaves (think burning newspaper).

3. **Synthetics (plastic-based):** Burns quickly and can continue to burn even if the flame is extinguished. Will melt and drip, forming plastic beads. Smoke is black and can be toxic; it has a chemical scent. Polyester is known for having a somewhat sweet scent along with the telltale chemical one.

TECHNIQUES

Along with base materials, you will also come across terms that describe the way the overall motif was applied to the garment. Depending on the complexity and, if possible, knowing who made the garment, the techniques can have a stronger influence on value than the fabric alone.

Yuzen (友禅): A laborious process of dyeing and painting that involves applying dye-resist paste to the areas that will not be dyed, coloring specific sections and motifs one at a time, rinsing it off in flowing water, and repeating for every color until the entire garment is finished. There are currently two main types of yuzen practiced in Japan: **kyo yuzen** (京友禅) from Kyoto and **kaga yuzen** (加賀友禅) from Kanagawa. Kyo yuzen is said to be very stylized, while kaga yuzen tends to depict subjects in a more bingata-like style.

Tsutsugaki (筒型): Also known as "**the cheap man's yuzen**," it uses a stickier (and less expensive) rice paste as a resist and is traditionally used on materials that were restricted to commoners, such as cotton or hemp. It is often used with indigo dye known as *aizome* (藍染).

Bingata (紅型: "**red stencil**"): A type of resist dyeing pioneered on the far southern island of Okinawa, it features a stencil to create a repeating pattern across the entire garment. The colors are filled in much like with woodblock prints, with a separate stencil used for each color. Bingata is noted for using almost every color of the rainbow on each garment, and even the most simple bingata kimono can take weeks to produce.

Katazome (型染): A stencil-dyeing technique that is very similar to bingata but was developed on the main islands of Japan. Unlike bingata, it traditionally used only cheaper or more affordable dyes such as indigo and was used mostly for the clothes of common people.

Shibori (絞り: "**tie-dyeing**"): Originally used by common people to decorate their clothing, it was dyed with natural indigo, which produced vibrant and striking patterns to otherwise plain garments. Ropes, threads, elastic, etc. are tied or sewn around a piece of fabric in certain ways so that, when dipped into a vat of dye, the bindings will resist the dye and remain blank. The process is very precise and laborious but produces extravagant patterns that are a feast for the eyes. It is extremely time consuming, but the effects are brilliant and closely tied to nature. Popular types of shibori include:

Kanoko (鹿の子: "**deer fawn**"): Small, square-looking areas that are meant to resemble the spots on young deer fawn. It is made by tying small elastic bands or thread onto the fabric and then dyeing.

Itajime (板締め: "**tightening boards**"): Folding or pleating the fabric before applying elastic bands or rope to resist the dye. It is then pressed between wooden boards while the fabric is submerged in the dye.

Arashi (嵐: "**storm**"): The cloth is first wrapped around a pole and then tied with the resistant strings or elastic before being dipped into the dye. This produces a diagonal pattern that can have great variation in color gradation. It gets its name from the strong colors and patterns, which resemble a thunderstorm.

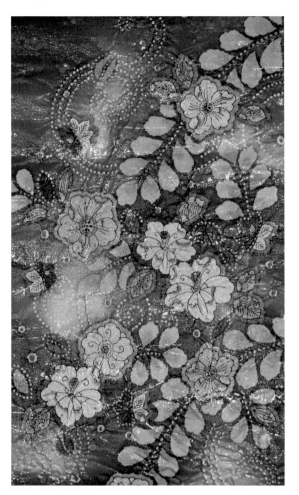

Tsujigahana (辻が花: "**trailing flowers**"): A specialized form of shibori that includes other decorative techniques to produce a piece of unsurpassed beauty. It was considered a lost art form until Itchiku Kubota, a man who spent decades trying to reproduce the technique and did not complete his study until he was sixty years old, revived it in the late twentieth century and blurred the lines between kimono as a garment and kimono as a work of art on an international level. It combines hand painting, dye resist painting, embroidery, and various tie-dye techniques to create patterns on a kimono that are made up of small flowers that flow across the garment in a sweeping effect that looks as though the flowers are trailing down from a plant. Due to its laborious nature, it can take up to two years to produce a single tsujigahana piece, but the process is being made cheaper by involving entire groups of people into the decorating process instead of a single artisan completing all the techniques by themselves.

Meisen (銘仙): A weave style that uses predyed woven threads known as **kasuri** (飛白: literally "**jumping white**") to weave intricate patterns and designs. Up close, the design seems very scattered and almost pixelated, but from a distance this technique produces fabulous patterns that are very eye-catching and striking when worn. Meisen-style garments became popular in the 1920s but had all but disappeared by the 1960s.

Urushi (漆: "**lacquer**"): A shellac that threads are dipped in, usually metallic or high-gloss colors, before being woven into a garment. The effect can be seen from far away and draws attention to the wearer.

Tsume tsuzure (爪綴れ: "**nail weaving**"): A style of weave that uses a person's fingernails on a loom for very fine and precise designs. It is incredibly labor intensive, and it can take a very long time to finish one motif, so the majority of tsuzure motifs are found on obi.

Tsumugi (紬: "**pongee**"): A weaving style with very thin threads that consists of many knots. For the most part it was used by workers and farmers and is still considered proper to use for informal kimono. There is an exceptionally fine tsumugi known as "**yuki tsumugi**" (結城紬) that fetches a very high price since it is one of the Important Intangible Cultural Properties of Japan and also an entry on the UNESCO Representative List of the Intangible Cultural Heritage of Humanity.

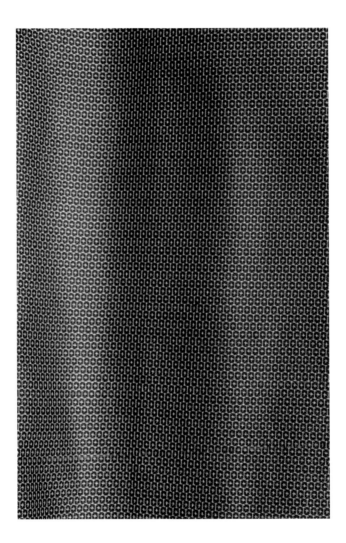

Omeshi chirimen (御召ちりめん: "**chirimen summons clothing**"): A weaving style that uses chirimen (thick crepe) silk for its base. It was traditionally used on high-quality garments of the imperial court and can be found on older formal kimono.

Chapter 4
Underwear: Juban and Donuki

A *juban* (襦袢), or "underwear," is a false kimono worn underneath the main kimono and against the skin to protect a kimono from perspiration. A juban peeks out slightly from the sleeves and hem, giving the impression that multiple kimono are being worn. Over a thousand years ago, during the Heian period, it was common to wear multiple kimono to flaunt one's wealth. This practice endured and can be found in every period that has come after, with minimal variations. During the Edo period, limits were placed on the various social classes concerning how many kimono could be worn and how ornate the patterns could be. In the late 1800s, this practice of wearing multiple kimono was abandoned in favor of buying Western wear. However, a juban continues to perpetuate the style of a second kimono at a fraction of the cost.

The defining feature of a woman's juban that separates it from a kimono is its collar. Ranging from completely plain to incredibly ornate, collars known as *eri* (襟/衿) are sewn with simple stitches onto the collar of a juban so that they will be visible when worn with the outer kimono. These collars act as an accessory and can add extra bursts of colors or textures to the outer kimono. Since eri are easy to swap out, it's common to have a large collection of eri but only a few juban. Most older juban and newer formal juban are made of silk, whereas many new and casual juban are made from synthetic fibers, such as polyester, which are easier to wash and take care of than their silken counterparts.

A Late Showa–period pink female juban
(*left*) and a blue male juban (*right*)
$40–$50 each

Defining features of a juban are as follows:

	MALE JUBAN	FEMALE JUBAN
Color	Cool, earthy tones such as brown, blue, black, or gray.	Red for younger children and unmarried women, pink and white for married or mature women. Modern ones can be any color.
Pattern	Motifs or scenes are painted on the back and are meant to be viewed only by the owner.	Has the same repeating pattern overall that tends to be woven instead of dyed.
Material	Mainly silk, with new ones being made from synthetic fibers.	Same as a male juban.
Number of Pieces	One single piece that looks like a kimono.	Can be one piece that covers the entire length (*nagajuban*: 長襦袢) or two pieces, one for the top (*hanjuban*: 半襦袢) and one for the skirt (*susoyoke*: 裾除け).
Collar	Collar is the same color as the juban or plain black.	Collar is white and allows the wearer to sew eri onto it to change its looks.

Remember: if the piece has a white collar, then you are dealing with a woman's juban. It is meant to have eri sewn on to change its look, and they are always plain so that unwanted patterns are not visible under the eri, creating a nice, clean look. A woman's juban will also have sleeves open both at the wrists and the underarms to help the wearer put on their main kimono properly. If the juban has motifs painted on the back between the shoulders, then you are dealing with a men's juban.

Most men and women will also wear an extra T-shirt-like top known as a ***hadajuban*** (肌襦袢) to protect their juban from perspiration. Because it will likely get dirty, hadajuban are made from washable fabrics such as cotton or polyester. It looks similar to a hanjuban, but the sleeves are form fitting and they are often white instead of colored. Oddly enough, men's hadajuban often have black collars, so look for this defining feature if you're trying to figure out what type of undergarment you have.

A hanjuban and susoyoke
$50

A ***donuki*** (胴抜), meaning "undergarment (to be worn in layers)," is a kimono meant to be worn under the main kimono; it has complementary patterns to match the main kimono but only at the parts of the garment that peek out from underneath. It resembles a juban, but the areas of the juban that line it and peek out are purposefully patterned to give the illusion of a second, fully patterned kimono for a fraction of the price. This was the early-twentieth-century style of layering kimono that was typically worn by nobility or brides underneath their main uchikake. Newer donuki are made for stage or performance purposes to mimic older fashion styles and are no longer produced for normal wear.

A yellow Late Showa–
period donuki
$50

EXCEPTIONS TO THE RULE

Kasane (襲/重ね: layering sets): In some extravagant cases, the donuki used for layering were full kimono and could be worn in their own right, apart from the main kimono. Whether they were just a donuki or a full kimono meant for layering, these sets were often composed of three kimono that followed this pattern:

1. Inner layer: Closest to the juban. Always the longest, since it would peek out from under the other layers, mostly at the skirt. The color was almost always white or cream colored as a symbol of purity.

2. Middle layer: Between the inner and outer layers. It would show in all the same places as the inner layer but would be slightly shorter by a few centimeters to allow for all layers to be seen. Colors from this layer were usually red or orange, because those are auspicious colors, but the layers being blue was not unheard of.

3. Outer layer: The one worn on the outside, which usually has the most decoration. Since this one will be seen by everyone, it is the most ornate—the most amount of work and detail is put into this one. It is the shortest of the three, to allow for the other two to peek out at the hems. This layer was black, since it denoted the highest formality possible.

Date eri (伊達衿: "showing-off eri"): A special type of eri that is clipped or sewn directly onto the lining of a kimono to give the illusion that the wearer is currently wearing more kimono than they really are. Unlike a normal eri, a date eri is worn only on formal kimono, such as furisode or tomesode, when a person is trying to express the greatest amount of importance or wealth.

KIMONO-WEARING SUPPLIES

Various items are needed to wear a kimono properly. All items are hidden underneath the kimono so that they are not seen when worn.

Kimono-wearing supplies include:

Koshihimo (腰紐: "waist ties"): The ties that actually bind the kimono onto a person. They are also used to hold the juban on.

Datejime (伊達締め: "showing-off tie"): This is used to hold the kimono on the person over the top of the koshihimo to provide a smooth look before applying the obi.

Eri shin (衿芯: "eri core"): A stiff piece of fabric inserted under the eri of the kimono to keep the collar in place

Korin belt (コーリンベルト): A special belt that keeps the juban collar straight and in line with the kimono

Chapter 5
Outerwear: Haori, Michiyuki, and More

In contrast to the length of sleeves and presence of a collar, a kimono jacket is much easier to identify than a type of kimono. Oftentimes they are so easy to identify as being a Japanese garment that people mistake them for children's kimono. Unlike a children's kimono, however, all types of kimono jackets will have a collar that extends the full length of the garment. And unlike a kimono, an unfinished jacket is known as a *karieba* (仮絵羽), which means "temporary haori."

Each type serves its own function and purpose, with the three never crossing into the realm of the other. They are as follows:

Haori (羽織: "**woven feathers**"): The most common type of kimono outerwear. Its name is a reference to the story of Hagoromo, a coat of feathers that allowed the gods to fly. It is characterized by its length, which goes down to one's hip (or longer for antique ones), its short sleeves, and its inability to close or allow one side to be folded over the other. The point of a haori is not to completely cover up your kimono, but rather to be able to show it off slightly before finally revealing it when you take the haori off. There are ties that go across the front of the haori to keep it lightly fastened so that the haori does not move out of place when walking. These *haori himo* (羽織紐: "**haori ties**") attach to small loops on the inside of the haori's collar. These ties can be as simple as two silk cords that are tied together or as fancy as a string of jade or coral beads. If your garment has these loops present, it is a sure sign that you have a haori. Haori are worn either as a jacket to help keep the wearer warm, or as an additional accessory to an outfit. A haori can be as simple as a solid color or as elaborate and ornate as having two complete sides that can be worn inside out from each other. When a haori contains two different designs like this, it is known as "*musou*" (無双).

A magenta Early Showa–period
haori with a brilliant peacock
$500

Michiyuki (道行: "**traveling wear**"): Like a longer haori, with one major difference: a michiyuki contains an extra panel of fabric that is meant to cover the middle portion left open by a haori. While this may seem like a fashion preference, it is actually the way in which a michiyuki distinguishes itself from a haori when it comes to its main purpose; while a haori is meant to be an accessory, a michiyuki is meant to be a raincoat. The extra panel over the front makes sure that the kimono underneath is fully protected from rain or snow, which would otherwise damage the silk of the kimono. There is another garment called a ***dochugi*** (道中着: **literally "along-the-way wear"**) that acts like a michiyuki for blocking out the elements, but it does not have an additional panel of fabric and just folds over the chest, to be done up by ties.

A multicolored Late Showa–
period michiyuki
$50–75

Happi (法被: "**working coat**"): Very much akin to jackets worn in Western civilizations. The most obvious trait is that the sleeves are form fitting and do not hang down like those on a kimono. Traditionally, happi were worn by servants, who had the kamon of their master printed on their happi to identify them when out in public. Nowadays happi are worn by participants in summer festivals, especially those whose jobs include heavy lifting and teamwork. They are further characterized by their striking black collars. Happi are incredibly informal and are usually made of cotton or hemp.

Some additional variations and subcategories of jackets include:

Hanten (半纏: "**half wrap**"): Almost identical in structure to a happi but padded on the inside for winter wear

Nenneko (ねんねこ): A mix between a haori and a hanten, it is a special jacket traditionally worn by mothers while carrying their babies on their backs. Today, it makes breastfeeding more convenient while wearing a kimono.

Kappōgi (割烹着: "**cooking wear**"): A special apron to protect kimono from spills and stains while cooking. It is tied in the back like a hospital gown.

Kataginu (肩衣): A traditional shoulder covering worn by men that attaches to the hakama to form an outfit known as a *kamishimo* (裃). In older times, these were used in lieu of a haori and were worn by male nobility and samurai. Unlike the haori, the kataginu offered a wider range of mobility. New kataginu are usually made for costume purposes, since the haori replaced the kataginu as the de facto clothing for formal occasions.

SPECIAL JACKETS FOR CHILDREN

For important shrine visits or formal events, many children wear a vest known as a *hifu* (被布). It is meant to protect the kimono from getting dirty—after all, young children do tend to have a knack for attracting stains.

A green Late Showa–period hifu
with flowers and butterflies
$50

Chapter 6
Bottoms: Hakama

Hakama (袴: **"divided skirt"**) are the kimono equivalent of pants. They are worn traditionally by men over a kimono to allow for ease of mobility. Showing any skin underneath a kimono is a cultural faux pas, so the hakama allows for a person to wear a kimono in public while retaining their dignity.

Hakama are iconic in samurai movies and pictures, because they allowed the wearer a full range of motion that could not be achieved by the stiff, tubelike kimono alone. Although they are routinely referred to as pants, hakama come in two different types: divided and undivided.

This garment gets its name from the pleats that are present in both types. Every pair of hakama has seven pleats—five in the front and two in the back—that are meant to represent the seven virtues of *bushido*. Meaning "way of the warrior," bushido has long been held as a code of honor for the warrior class in Japan. The seven virtues are justice, courage, mercy, respect, honesty, honor, and loyalty.

The divided type, known as *umamori* (馬乗り), literally "horse-riding pants," are very much like divided pants and were originally worn to protect a person's legs while riding horses, making them popular among the samurai class. The undivided hakama, called *andon bakama* (行灯袴), literally "lantern pants," are worn for almost any situation at any level of formality. Hakama are becoming increasingly popular with women because of their flexibility. Some young girls wear furisode with hakama to their school graduation ceremonies.

A Heisei-period set of women's andon bakama
with blue-and-red gradation
$75–$100

Chapter 7
Belts: Obi

Although not worn like a kimono, an **obi** (帯), "belt," is a piece of cloth that secures the kimono to the wearer. Originally, obi were nothing more than simple ties to keep the many-layered kimono together, but over time they evolved into an independent entity that comes in many different shapes and sizes to suit the occasion. Just like kimono, obi are made in a wide variety of materials, lengths, and formalities, but this chapter will help you navigate them all with ease. Note that the majority of obi types are worn by women, much like kimono, so if the obi is also used by men, that will be noted in the description.

Anatomy of an Obi

Tesaki (手先): The "start" of an obi. It has no special markings and has the same pattern as the rest of the obi.

Domawari (胴回り): The "waist" section, which will be seen at the front/waist of a person when worn

Oridashi (織り出し): A woven line that marks the end/bottom of an obi

Taresaki (たれ先): The "end" or "bottom" of an obi. It is just below the oridashi.

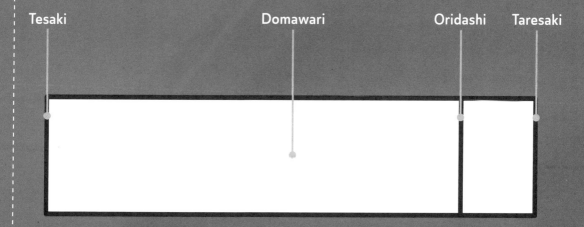

Tesaki   Domawari   Oridashi   Taresaki

FULL-WIDTH OBI

These obi have "standardized" sizes to be worn with almost any type of kimono. Each is approximately 30 centimeters (12 inches) wide and 300–400 centimeters (118–157 inches) long. Older obi tend to be shorter than newer examples because the latter are lengthened to make more ornate styles of knots.

Maru obi (丸帯): "**Circle or repeating obi**" are double-sided, fully patterned obi that usually have some type of motif or scene repeated along the entire length. The term *maru* refers to being able to line up the ends of the obi and have the pattern continue infinitely like a circle. Because of their high cost of production, very few maru obi are made today, so almost every maru obi that you come across is a vintage or antique piece.

An Early Showa–period maru obi
featuring drums, waves, and pine
$75–$100.

Fukuro obi (袋帯): "**Sack obi**" are heavily patterned like maru obi but have the pattern on only 60 percent of the garment. The other 40 percent is plain and matches the color of the obi's base. A fukuro obi is meant to look and act like a maru obi, but it comes at a fraction of the cost, since it is not fully patterned. Some fukuro obi will be entirely blank on one side, with decoration on the other. These came into being before World War II but did not become popular until the 1950s. By then, it had replaced maru obi as the most formal style, and it is still produced today.

A Late Showa–period gold fukuro obi featuring stylized flowers
$50–$75

Chuya obi (典雅帯): "**Night and day obi**" are full-length obi that have different patterns and motifs on each side. Some might have similar motifs on both sides, but most have distinctly different motifs with different colors. The bulk of chuya obi were made prior to World War II, when maru obi were still being produced. Some artisans are still making chuya obi, albeit shorter than a standard maru or fukuro obi.

A Heisei-period chuya obi with a pattern of gold and black flowers on one side and multicolored flowers with auspicious motifs on the other
$75–$100

Heko obi (兵児帯): "**Soft obi**" are worn by men with casual clothing, such as yukata, or by young boys. The fabric is soft and easy to tie, which allows children to learn how to fasten the knots of their obi properly. Since this obi is seen as something that men grow out of, it is appropriate to wear only with very informal clothing.

A Late Showa–period dark-blue heko obi
$50

Exceptions to the Rule

Hikinuki obi (引き抜き帯): "**Quick-change obi**" are full-length obi (usually maru) that have patterns printed facing the wrong way / upside down. These obi are traditionally used by geisha and kabuki performers because they tie their obi in a special knot that turns the pattern right side up when worn.

A Late Showa–period hikinuki obi featuring red wisteria
$50–$75

THE HYBRID OBI

Nagoya obi (名古屋帯): "**Nagoya-style obi**" is a hybrid type that is part full length and part half length. The parts that will be made into the knot and will be seen from the back are full width, but the parts in the front are either half width or sewn together for ease of wear. A Nagoya obi is much easier to put on than a maru or fukuro obi, but it is meant to be tied in only one style of knot, known as a "taiko" (literally "drum"). While it is possible to tie a Nagoya obi into other styles of knots, its main design is for that of the taiko-style knot. A Nagoya obi is worn with a casual kimono such as a komon, iromuji, or tsukesage but never with something as formal as a furisode, houmongi, or tomesode.

An orange Late Showa–period Nagoya obi
with stylized flowers
$50

HALF-WIDTH OBI

Hanhaba obi (半幅帯): A "**half-width obi**" is, as its name suggests, half the width of a full-size obi. A hanhaba obi is approximately 15 centimeters (6 inches) wide and 300–400 centimeters (118–157 inches) long. These obi also have standardized sizes, but since they are worn casually and cannot be tied in elaborate knots, they tend to be quite simple and even homemade. These obi are for informal wear, including komon or yukata, and they are thinner than a full-size obi to allow for faster tying.

Kaku obi (角帯): "**Stiff obi**" are worn by grown men. As the name suggests, they are slightly stiffer than heko obi but hold their shape well and present a crisp and clean look when tied.

A beige Early Showa–period hanhaba obi with a wisteria maiden motif
$50

A brown Late Showa–period kaku obi
$40–$50

Exception to the Rule

Tsuke (付け), translated as "fixed," are obi that are pretied; they require little effort to put on but give the effect of a fully tied obi. Most casual tsuke obi are made of polyester for easy upkeep, but there are some formal fukuro-/maru-style obi that are made from old obi. They are great for people who have difficulty tying knots or for someone who is new to wearing kimono. There is much debate surrounding whether tsuke obi, even ones made from maru and fukuro obi, can be worn to formal functions, since tsuke obi are seen as "cheap" due to their easy-to-wear construction.

A yellow Heisei-period tsuke obi showing both the knot and waist parts
$50

The most commonly made tsuke obi are for:

Yukata: One long piece for the waist and another fashioned into a butterfly knot that hooks onto the waist part. The material for this is usually simple silk or polyester due to its lack of formality.

Children: A long piece for the waist and an ornate style of knot that is decorated with little charms. The type of obi that this is simulating is either a maru or fukuro obi, since these obi are worn on special occasions.

Casual wear: Almost always in the taiko (drum) style like a Nagoya obi, this version gives the look of a simple obi and requires barely any effort to put on. They tend to feature simple patterns and the same parts as tsuke obi for yukata.

Types of Obi and When They Should Be Worn

	FULL WIDTH	HALF WIDTH	FORMAL WEAR	CASUAL WEAR
Maru Obi	✓	—	✓	—
Fukuro Obi	✓	—	✓	—
Chuya Obi	✓	✓	✓	✓
Nagoya Obi	✓	✓	—	✓
Hanhaba Obi	—	✓	—	✓
Heko Obi	✓	—	—	✓
Kaku Obi	—	✓	✓	—
Tsuke Obi	✓	✓	✓	✓

SPECIAL OBI

Maiko darari obi: *Maiko* (舞妓: literally "woman of dance") are apprentice geisha who were often found in the southern parts of Japan but are now exclusively in Kyoto, Nara, Nagoya, and Gifu. Those in Kyoto and Nara maintain the tradition of wearing extra-long obi known as ***darari obi*** (だらりの帯), literally "dangling obi," which are over 600 centimeters (236 inches) long. Besides their impressive length, they are marked at the end with the kamon of the maiko's *okiya*, the place where they live and train. They can be decorated in either the maru, fukuro, or chuya styles. They are extremely rare and thus often fetch very high prices from collectors.

Iwata obi (岩田帯) or **hara obi** (腹帯): A special loose obi that is approximately the same size as a hanhaba obi but is made of much softer material. It is used by women so that they can still wear kimono while pregnant; they give some much-needed lower-back support to the soon-to-be mother. They can be found under the names *iwata obi* (iwata-styled obi) or *hara obi* (maternity obi).

An orange Late Showa–period darari obi with climbing ivy
$500–$750

OBI ACCESSORIES

Similar to kimono, obi have accessories that must be used in order for the obi to be worn properly.

Obi ita (帯板: "obi board"): A flat board that goes between the layers of the obi in the front to keep them flat against the wearer

Obi makura (帯枕: "obi pillow"): A soft pillow that holds the obi up in the back to give it shape. They are most often used with Nagoya obi.

Obiage (帯揚げ: "obi raiser"): A piece of cloth that covers the obi makura and helps keep the obi up at the back. It is tucked into the front of the obi, with a small bit peeking out for a pop of color.

Obijime (帯締め: "obi tie"): A cord tied around the obi to hold it in place, depending on the obi knot used or just as a decoration

Obidome (帯留め: "obi fastener"): An accessory that is slid onto the obijime to provide additional decoration to an outfit. The name comes from a time when the obidome acted like belt buckles and held the obijime together.

A set of obi-wearing accessories,
including an obi ita, obi makura,
obiage, obijime, and obidome

Part II

Chapter 8
Dating a Kimono

At first it may be hard to identify how old your kimono is or to know what determines its value, but looking at the patterns used by kimono artisans over the decades should sort out the majority of your questions. This chapter will explain what to look out for to determine age and value.

TIME PERIODS

Since kimono are made from cloth, it is rare to find one that is more than a hundred years old. Nevertheless, many antique kimono did find their way into Western culture, brought back as presents from Japan during the Allied occupation and stored away in drawers ever since. The majority of these kimono were precious heirlooms that Japanese families sold off to GIs to keep themselves from starving. It is not unheard of, therefore, to find a rare kimono among old items forgotten in attics and basements.

To determine how old your kimono is, you will need to match it with similar styles of appliqué, since fashion trends follow specific and traceable patterns over time. Here are the major historical eras and the things to look for when determining age.

The Meiji Period (明治時代): 1867–1912

The oldest kimono found in Western markets date back to the time when Japan was rapidly modernizing itself to compete on an international level with other countries. While Western dress was encouraged, many Japanese still owned kimono, although only the best of this period have survived. The kimono that you find from this period were owned by the wealthiest families, since they were kept in special containers and given much more reverence than daily clothes. The majority of pieces from this time are uchikake, which were owned both by nobles and wedding-goers alike. In the Edo period it was common for kimono to have motifs only within a single panel like a tsukesage, but the Meiji period began to see the rise of kimono being a single piece that flows together.

There are two major types of kimono found during this time can be identified:

Wedding: Usually covered in a combination of cranes, plum blossoms, bamboo, pine needles, waves, and turtles (all auspicious motifs) that were embroidered onto the garment

Formal: Had decoration only along the bottom hem in a wide variety of motifs

The biggest indicators of age for this period are the materials, specifically gold and silk, and how they were applied. The majority will feature actual gold, which is wrapped around a thin thread and then woven onto garments as either an accent or overall decoration. A special type of silk known as *shusu* was popular during this time; it had a satin-like shine that was very eye-catching. Most wedding kimono were made with either black, white, or red silk, with some made in blue. Kamon were also slightly larger than average during this time, since identifying families through their crests was still very important. All the linings on these kimono were made of silk that was dyed using saffron flowers. Because saffron was so hard to come by, this dye was the ultimate show of wealth, and the color was very lucky and auspicious. This type of dye is known as **benibana** (紅花), which translates to "crimson flowers." The padding on these kimono was also very large since they were meant to be worn trailing on the ground.

Things to Look For

Shusu silk

Very large kamon

Gold thread

Heavy embroidery

Thick padding

Benibana lining

A black Meiji-period uchikake featuring
cranes and auspicious plants
$2,500

The Taisho Period (大正時代): 1912–1926

This period saw the most change and offers some of the best examples of kimono as art. During this time, Japan became an economic powerhouse, and with that development came the creation of many kimono. Styles did not stay static for long, and as the period moved on, so did the amount of Western influence on the garment.

Early Taisho kimono have slightly smaller kamon compared to their Meiji counterparts, and most traded the massive amounts of embroidery for beautiful hand-painted masterpieces. The motifs have a soft look and appear to almost glow. A special type of motif placement known as *ryōzuma* (両褄, literally "mirror pattern") became popular on formal kimono, which featured identical or nearly identical motifs painted on the outside panels (as well as the bottom of furisode sleeves) while leaving the inside ones blank. This mirrored pattern was visible only from the front, so one had to engage the wearer in conversation to take in the full effect.

Around this time, Japan was adopting Western furniture along with fashion, which brought about another significant change in kimono decoration. It is around this time that you see patterns being placed on the shoulders of kimono. When seated at a traditional Japanese table, the full view of the kimono was always visible; with the adoption of tall tables and chairs, however, it became almost impossible to see the kimono motifs while the wearer was seated. Thus, adding motifs on the shoulders allowed for small patterns to be visible and allowed for a greater sense of imagination, since you knew that the motifs on the shoulders were just miniature versions of the ones along the skirt.

In the Middle Taisho period, a major shift in style occurred, a result of the adoption of Western ideals and practices by Japanese people. Motifs become more solid and even begin to incorporate foreign subjects. Kimono with this style are known as "Taisho Roman." The meaning is taken directly from the city of Rome and uses the term "Roman" to denote its Western influence. By the Late Taisho period, the two previous styles blended together, but the Western influence was still favored over all.

This is also the height of luxurious patterns woven into the silk, known as *rinzu* (綸子, "figured silk"). Rinzu was practiced before the Taisho period, but it became an art unto itself during the kimono boom of this time. Rinzu used to be small, repeating patterns woven into silk that added an extra bit of luxuriance to a kimono (and is still practiced today), but during this time, the patterns became larger and were able to be seen from a distance. The woven patterns were equal in opulence to the main painted motifs and would continue in this manner until the Second World War.

Compared to contemporary kimono, the kimono of the Taisho period had slightly longer sleeves. The benibana-dyed lining also fell out of vogue, with the introduction of synthetic dyes to Japan; this led to people wanting a lining for their kimono that was a bright, striking, and uniform red. Benibana varied from a dark orange to a light red, but it never achieved a true crimson. Synthetic dyes from the West also drastically lowered the cost and made red lining available to everyone, regardless of wealth. The black dyes used during this period, however, were not very good in standing the test of time; almost all Taisho pieces made from this black are faded in some way and are now seen as a brown color. Synthetic and better natural mixes would fix this problem by the Showa period. Linings for haori were bright and colorful, with motifs that were usually related to those on the outside of the garment.

Things to Look For

Soft, glowing motifs

Ryōzuma pattern

Painterly designs

Motifs on shoulders

Woven rinzu fabrics

Western motifs or styles

Faded black dye

A green Taisho-period furisode
with peacocks and flowers
$250–$300

The Showa Period (昭和時代): 1926–1989

Since the Showa period lasted almost sixty-four years, it is best to break it into two sections. Kimono varied over such a long period, with the most drastic changes occurring before and after World War II.

The Early Showa Period: 1926–1945

In the Early Showa, the red-lined kimono continued to be popular, and almost all female kimono were lined with red. The painterly designs of the Taisho were completely replaced with bold and very colorful pieces, which seemed to become more Western-like as time went on. This, however, changed prior to World War II, when Japan became a nation steeped in imperialism and saw kimono keeping only native Japanese motifs and shunning foreign ideas and designs. Many items were produced with war themes, which included planes, soldiers, and Japanese flags. The war was very costly, and kimono production slowed drastically by 1943, with very few pieces being made in the next ten years relative to previous output.

Things to Look For

Bold, flat designs

Dark-black dyes

Red lining

War/imperial themes

A white Early Showa–period furisode
with peacocks and ships
$250–$300

The Late Showa Period: 1945–1989

The longer of the two eras, the Late Showa period saw the most drastic change when it came to kimono. During the American occupation from 1945 to 1947, Japan was modernizing and distancing itself from its past to forge a better future. This, sadly, meant that the kimono market did not rebound like it had from previous wars. The kimono went from being a daily-wear item to something seen only during formal occasions. Japanese designs were often shunned in favor of Western-style designs, such as arabesque, minimalist, or futuristic styles, with color schemes being akin those that were popular in Western fashion, albeit slightly gaudier and brighter. Looking at kimono from this time is like looking at a mirror of Western fashion. It is during this period that kimono became standardized, with sleeve length, width, and overall length becoming uniform in size and not varying as much as it did prior to the war. Sleeves were now shorter, overall kimono length was slightly longer, and padding was all but removed from hems (minus those on uchikake). Almost all instances of single or triple kamon on kimono were replaced with five, only due to the overall decreased production of kimono. The bold red linings were replaced by mostly cream or white linings, with some having a small amount of color on the edges that would fade into white or cream toward the center.

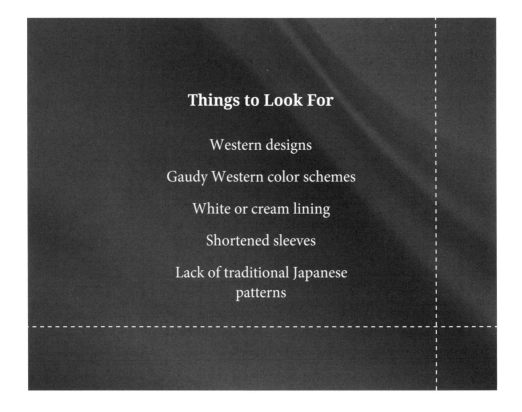

Things to Look For

Western designs

Gaudy Western color schemes

White or cream lining

Shortened sleeves

Lack of traditional Japanese
patterns

A multicolored Late Showa–period
furisode with shibori plum blossoms
$200–$250

The Heisei Period (平成時代): 1989–2019

The most recent era has been witness to a kimono renaissance that started in the early 1990s, when the bubble economy burst and Japan had to once again rebuild itself. Although kimono production continued to slow into the early 2000s, it is safe to say that it was saved by an unlikely companion: the internet. For the first time, the world—as well as the Japanese—could see the beauty of old kimono and the wonderful art that they had all but forgotten.

Colors and symbols on kimono returned to the traditional Japanese styles and colors, and new techniques of producing kimono have made them accessible to all skill levels and budgets. New materials such as polyester and rayon have made kimono wear and care easier than ever before, allowing them to be cleaned in a washing machine. The advent of mass production has also seen the emergence of new companies that are able to sell many different colors and styles of kimono without being affected by the time restrictions and availability of artisans. This is not to say that artisan kimono are no longer being produced, but mass production via screen or digital printing has made casual or beginner kimono available to everyone. Artisans are now actively signing their kimono with special stamps that bear their names; some even include tags like Western clothing.

It is also thanks to the internet that, with just a computer, people can find guides and tutorials explaining how to wear kimono and even how to make their own. This ease of access has led more Western people than ever before to collect and wear kimono, and many have formed online groups to help each other with coordinations and styles. The kimono has gone from a singular garment with a specific set of steps for wear to a piece that can be transformed into any style the wearer chooses, from goth and Lolita to casual, rock, and so many more.

Things to Look For

Synthetic materials

Artisan signatures or tags

Traditional Japanese designs and colors

Metallic/shiny threads for obi

Pop-culture symbols

A blue Heisei-period houmongi
with feathers
$100–150

The Reiwa Period (令和時代): 2019–Present

So far, not much has changed from the Heisei period, since the Reiwa is still in its infancy. Kimono made today still feature artisans trying new styles of motifs, and images of old woodblock heroes and heroines are taking center stage in the digital age of kimono printing.

Chapter 9
Determining Value

Kimono, like any other collectible, will always have certain traits that are more desirable to collectors. These traits will inevitably reduce or increase the value, depending on whether they are present on your garment or not, and they are the factors that will determine the value of your kimono. Examples shown are based on 2020 prices collected from numerous English and Japanese sources, including Ichiroya, LiveAuctioneers, Sou Japan, Yahoo! Japan Auctions, Etsy, and Ohio Kimono.

CONDITION

Appearance, quality, and overall wear and tear are by far the most important factors in determining value. Even if a kimono is very old and highly sought after, its value can be negatively affected or much diminished if it is full of holes or covered in stains. Since kimono are made of cloth, they do tend to break down over time, so condition is paramount when pricing your item or buying an example for your collection. If you can find little in the way of staining, tearing, or fading, then your item is in good or excellent condition and can command the highest price possible. If it is heavily damaged, then the price falls drastically, on the basis of how prominent and numerous the defects are.

A G E

As discussed, the older a kimono is, the higher the value it tends to command. That is not to say that all old kimono are automatically worth more than newer kimono, but certain examples, such as those from the Taisho period, are highly desirable because of the colors and designs characteristic of that era. For garments and fabrics, an item is considered vintage when it is twenty years old and antique at eighty years old (not one hundred, as is true for most antiques). Some unscrupulous sellers will attempt to assign their own dating system, so be on the lookout for items that are called "antique" but are only thirty or so years old.

MOTIFS

The decoration is likely the only trait that is not determined by a garment's age or condition. Even in modern kimono, certain themes remain rare and are highly sought after by collectors. Most tend not to fit into preconceived class or gender ideas; they break the mold of the traditional and turn it into something that only special and unique individuals would be able to wear. In most cases, it is safe to say that if something falls into a rarer category, then the price will be higher than for a simple, common theme.

On the following pages you will find lists of common, uncommon, and rare motifs to help you determine price and value.

Common Motifs

arabesque patterns or designs: karakusa (唐草)

bamboo: take (竹)

bell flowers: kikyō (桔梗)

butterflies: chō (蝶)

carp: koi (鯉) (on men's kimono)

celebratory paper strips: tabane noshi (束ね熨斗)

cherry blossoms: sakura (桜)

chrysanthemums: kiku (菊)

cranes: tsuru (鶴)

dragons: ryū (龍) (on men's kimono)

eagles: washi (鷲) (on men's kimono)

fans: sensu (扇子)

flower carts: hana guruma (花車)

grasses: shiba (柴)

hawks: taka (鷹) (on men's kimono)

hexagons: rokkaku (六角)

irises: ayame (菖蒲)

ivy: tsuta (蔦)

leaves: ha (葉)

lions: shishiko (猪子) (on men's kimono)

mandarin ducks: oshidori (鴛鴦)

maple leaves (green): kaede (楓)

maple leaves (colored): momiji (紅葉)

palanquins: gosho guruma (御所車)

paulownia: kiri (桐)

peacocks: kujaku (孔雀)

peonies: botan (牡丹)

phoenixes: ho-oh (鳳凰)

pine: matsu (松)

plum blossoms: ume (梅)

repeating geometric pattern: hakata (博多)

stripes: shima (縞)

stylized flowers: karabana (唐花)

tigers: tora (虎) (on men's kimono)

tortoiseshell pattern: kikkō (亀甲)

war helmets: kabuto (兜) (boys' kimono only)

waves: nami (波)

willow: yanagi (柳)

wisteria: fuji (藤)

woven balls: temari (手毬) (girls' kimono only)

An orange Late Showa–period
houmongi featuring chrysanthemums
$75–100

Uncommon Motifs

arrows: yabane (矢羽)
beautiful ladies: bijin (美人)
boats: fune (舟)
books: hon (本)
bridges: hashi (橋)
bush clover: hagi (萩)
camellia: tsubaki (椿)
carnations: nadeshiko (撫子)
clematis: tessen (鉄線)
clouds: kumo (雲)
daruma: 達磨
dolls: hina (雛)
fireworks: hanabi (花火)
fish: sakana (魚)
fish scales: uroko (鱗)
flower balls/bouquets: kusudama (薬玉)
grapes: budō (葡萄)
haze: kasumi (霞)
Heian-period ladies: Heian jidai onna (平安時代女)
hemp leaves: asanoha (麻の葉)
herons: sagi (鷺)
horses: uma (馬) (on men's kimono)
hydrangeas: ajisai (紫陽花)
insects: mushi (虫)
Japanese writing: kanji (漢字)
lilies: yuri (百合)
lobsters/shrimp: ebi (蝦)
lucky mallets: kizuchi (木槌)
magnolia: mokuren (木蓮)
morning glories: asagao (朝顔)

mountains: yama (山)

musical instruments: gakki (楽器)

orange blossoms: tachibana (橘)

orchids: ran (蘭)

pheasants: kiji (雉)

pine cones: matsuba (松葉)

plovers: chidori (千鳥)

roses: bara (薔薇)

round waves: seigaiha (青海波)

saddles: kura (鞍)

scrolls: makimono (巻き物)

seagulls: kamome (鴎)

seven treasures: shippō (七宝)

shells: kai (貝)

shell-matching game: kai awase (貝合わせ)

silk cords: kumihimo (組紐)

small children: karako (唐子)

snowflakes: yukiwa (雪和)

spinning tops: koma (こま)

swallows: tsubame (燕)

sunflowers: himawari (向日葵)

temples: shinden (神殿)

towns: sato (里)

turtles: kame (亀)

umbrellas: kasa (傘)

vases and jars: tsubo (壺) or hanabin (花瓶)

war motifs: sensō (戦争)

waterlilies: suiren (睡蓮)

waterwheels: suisha (水車)

wheels: sharin (車輪)

A black Late Showa–period hikizuri/
susohiki featuring beautiful women
$750–$1,000

Rare Motifs

azaleas: tsutsuji (筒状)

beaches: kishi (岸)

bells: suzu (鈴)

camels: rakuda (駱駝)

carp: koi (鯉) (on women's kimono)

cats: neko (猫)

cormorants: u (鵜)

cows or oxen: ushi (牛)

crows: karasu (烏)

daffodils: suiscn (水仙)

deer: shika (鹿)

dogs: inu (犬)

doves: hato (鳩)

dragons: ryū (龍) (on women's kimono)

eagles: washi (鷲) (on women's kimono)

Egyptian patterns or designs: Ejiputo teemu (エジプトテーマ)

elephants: zō (象)

feather cloak: Hagoromo (羽衣)

fire: hi (火)

fireflies: hotaru (蛍)

foxes: kitsune (狐)

frogs: kaeru (蛙)

geese: gachō (鵞鳥)

gods or deities: kami (神)

hair ornaments: kanzashi (簪)

hawks: taka (鷹) (on women's kimono)

horses: uma (馬) (on women's kimono)

kabuki characters: kabuki tōjōjinbutsu (歌舞伎登場人物)

lions: shishi (猪子) (on women's kimono)

lizards: tokage (蜥蜴)

lotus: hasu (蓮)

mallows or hibiscus: fuyō (芙蓉)

monkeys: saru (猿)

moon: tsuki (月)

nightingales: uguisu (鶯)

owls: fukurō (梟)

paper butterflies: orichō (織蝶)

paper cranes: orizuru (織鶴)

parrots: ōmu (鸚鵡)

peaches: momo (桃)

pigs: buta (豚)

planets: wakusei (惑星)

playing cards: toranpu (トランプ)

poppies: keshi (芥子)

rabbits: usagi (兎)

roosters and chickens: niwatori (鶏)

sheep or goats: hitsuji (羊)

ships with black sails: kurofune (黒船)

skeletons: kokkaku (骨格)

snakes: hebi (蛇)

sparrows: suzume (雀)

spiders: kumo (蜘蛛)

snow: yuki (雪)

swans: hakuchō (白鳥)

tigers: tora (虎) (on women's kimono)

treasure ships: takarabune (宝船)

tulips: chūrippu (チューリップ)

vegetables: yasai (野菜)

A mint-green Late Showa–period
houmongi with azaleas
$100–$150

EXECUTION AND TECHNIQUE

Certainly, the rarity of an item can push up its value, but you should never underestimate an artisan's skill in bringing even a common motif, such as a peacock, into a stunning piece worthy of a museum. Therefore, it is important to note how that motif came to be on your kimono and how its presence will either drive up or bring down the price. Here are some factors that affect a kimono and its motifs.

Factors That Lower Price

Basic weave	Synthetic fibers
Screen printing	Little or no decoration
Mass production	Patterns
Limited colors	

Factors That Raise Price

Real gold thread	Fancy fabrics (including summer kimono fabrics)
Patterns woven into fabric (rinzu)	
Embroidery	Intricate decoration (such as tsujigahana)
Master painting skills	

Note that kimono made from summer silks are worth more than their regular silk counterparts, because far fewer kimono were made for summer wear than for year-round wear. Yukata, however, are exempt from the summer rule since they are almost never made from silk.

TYPE OF KIMONO

As explained in earlier chapters, the different types of kimono and their corresponding level of formality will be essential in determining value. Typically, the lower the formality, the lower the value, since informal kimono are produced in much larger quantities than formal ones. Types of kimono by average value are as follows.

Level 5 (Most Expensive):
$150–$250+
uchikake
hikizuri/susohiki
darari obi

Level 4 (More Expensive):
$100–$150
furisode
kakeshita

Level 3 (Moderately Expensive):
$75–$100
houmongi
tsukesage
maru obi

Level 2 (Less Expensive):
$50–$75
hakama
fukuro obi
chuya obi

Level 1 (Least Expensive):
$50 and Under
tomesode*
iromuji
haori
michiyuki
mofuku
Edo komon
komon
yukata
juban
happi
hanten
tsuke obi
heko obi
kaku obi
Nagoya obi
hanhaba obi

*While tomesode have the highest level of formality, they are worn only once or twice in their lifetime, and used ones are very easy to find at low prices due to the multitudes of kimono makers who churn out new tomesode to constantly to keep up with popular designs. The vast majority of contemporary tomesode are not owned by regular people, but by kimono rental studios that rent them out for weddings, since the cost to buy a brand-new tomesode is very high, and most people do not want to spend so much on an item that they will wear only once or twice. This type of kimono also possess the least amount of decoration out of any other kimono type. Older tomesode of the Taisho, Meiji, and Edo periods are exempt from this low-value rating, since they are much more desirable by collectors for their exceptionally executed techniques and their overall rarity due to age.

Chapter 10

Documenting and Photographing Your Kimono

For the person who wants to sell kimono or to have photographs on hand for insurance purposes, there are some basic dos and don'ts that can make or break your presentation. Remember: if it can't be seen, then you will lose out on its value.

SETTING UP YOUR KIMONO

Determining how you plan to photograph your kimono, whether laying it down or hanging it up, is the first step. Try to find a blank wall or set up a plain background so that all focus will be on your kimono and not background items. Generally, it is best to take pictures of kimono while they are hanging and not when they are lying on the floor. Hanging displays the kimono as it should be worn, whereas lying it on a flat surface tends to distort the angle at which you are taking pictures, making some parts of the kimono look larger or smaller than they really are.

The best item to use for this is a kimono hanger. It resembles a regular coat hanger but has telescopic ends that stretch to support the kimono and its sleeves. They are relatively cheap (about $15 from Japan), but you could always attempt to make your own by using a wooden dowel instead.

Once you have your kimono hanging, you will need a way to keep it "fanned out" so that the maximum amount of the garment can be seen. Traditional wooden kimono stands have clips that would do this for you, but they can be quite expensive ($150 at minimum, but mostly higher). One of the easiest tricks is to use painter's tape to hold the kimono to the wall. **Do not use any other type of tape**, since it will leave residue or may pull dye from the fabric. You will want to keep the parts of the hem fanned out as far as the garment will allow without pulling. If the hem is pulling away from the tape, then it is too far out.

It is usually best to start by taking pictures of the back of the kimono first (where the majority of the decoration is) and then flipping it over to photograph the inside. The outside is what people will judge when they see the image, so take the time to get everything right. **I personally do not advocate for people keeping kimono as decorations on their walls, since it will only lead to the destruction of a valuable and treasured item.** However, this is a personal choice, and if you want to display it, then be sure to make sure that it is fully supported and kept out of direct sunlight.

THE PHOTOGRAPHY PROCESS

It's best to stand at least 10 feet (3 meters) away from the kimono to allow the camera to capture the entire garment. Natural lighting is always preferred, but if you need to use fluorescent lighting, then make sure to have some sort of flash guard to avoid blowing out your images. Use the camera's macro mode to document tears or stains as well as any small parts that you feel are important (such as kamon or maker's marks). Once you've done all of that, flip the kimono over and do the same for the inside. Remember: you can never have too much documentation.

MEASURING

While you have your kimono out, now is the best time to take detailed measurements that will allow you to clearly identify what type of kimono (or obi) you have. This information will also help potential buyers or appraisers know how big or small the garment is.

The places to measure include the following:

Length: Length is measured from the top of the collar to the very bottom of the hem. This is called the *mitake* (身丈).

Width / Arm Span: Width is measured across the back, from the end of one sleeve to the other. Since kimono are dynamic pieces, it is best to describe the width as the "arm span" and reserve the word *width* for obi only. The length from the sleeve to the back seam is called the *yuki* (裄).

Sleeve Length: This is an incredibly important measurement since it is one of the best indicators of kimono type. It is pertinent to know that, on average, sleeve length was slightly longer before World War II, so antique or vintage pieces will have longer sleeves compared to their contemporary counterparts.

Exception to the Rule

Since happi are meant to have form-fitting sleeves, they do not require a measurement for sleeve length. Similarly, susoyoke, which are meant to be worn from the waist down, do not contain sleeves, so it is also not listed under sleeve length.

EDITING YOUR IMAGES

Here is where you will choose the photographs that you feel show off your kimono at its finest. You will likely need to do some cropping and color-correcting to ensure that the kimono in your pictures looks just as it does in real life, but do not delete or cover any defects. Being honest is far more beneficial than trying to cover up blemishes, a practice that will only hurt your reputation as a seller. Defects are a normal part of any kimono, and they make each one unique, so don't feel discouraged if yours has a spot or smudge.

For those who want to sell on a professional or semiprofessional level, it is a good idea to add a watermark to your images, which will help prevent them from being stolen and posted on other websites without your permission.

Another tip: back up your images to a cloud service. It is better to be safe than sorry, and having copies of images separate from your computer's hard drive will help ensure that you always have access to your photographs wherever you go.

STORING YOUR KIMONO

As with any object, how you store it is tantamount to keeping it in the best condition possible. Sadly, there are many kimono that have been ruined from improper storage that go up for sale each year, and the owners are not aware of the inadvertent damage that they have caused to the garment. Most of this damage is caused by putting kimono on clothing hangers; the stress from the hanger causes the fabric to thin and, if left hanging for a long time, will eventually make the sleeves fall off!

To preserve the garment, it is always best to fold your kimono and other garments for storage. Kimono are designed to be easily folded by following a series of steps. First, lay the kimono flat out with the inside lining facing up. Then:

1. Fold the first panel of the outer layers into the center with the left side reaching the middle.

2. Fold the top part of the left side back by one panel.

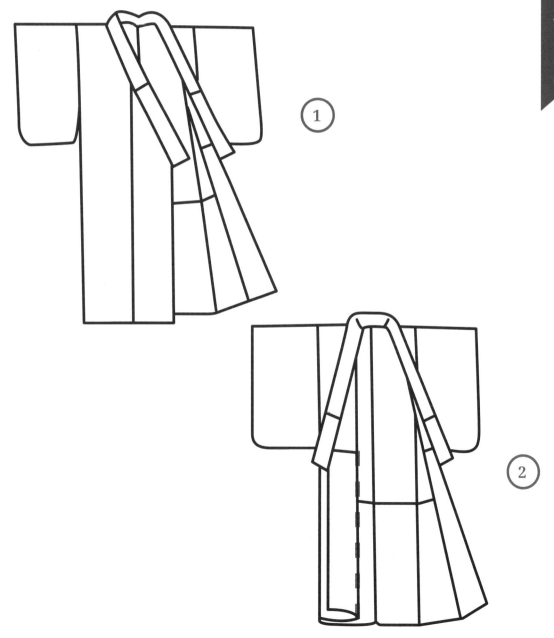

3. Fold in the top part of the collar.

4. Fold the right side over to meet the left side collar.

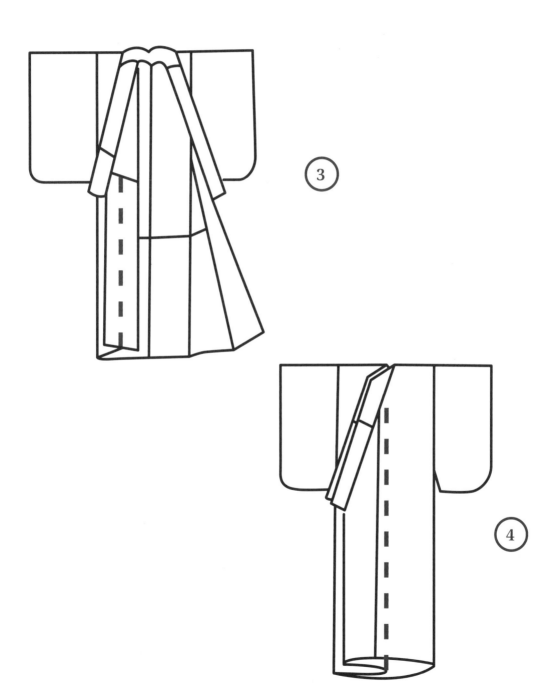

5. Fold the sleeves over to meet each other.

6. Fold the right sleeve back onto the kimono.

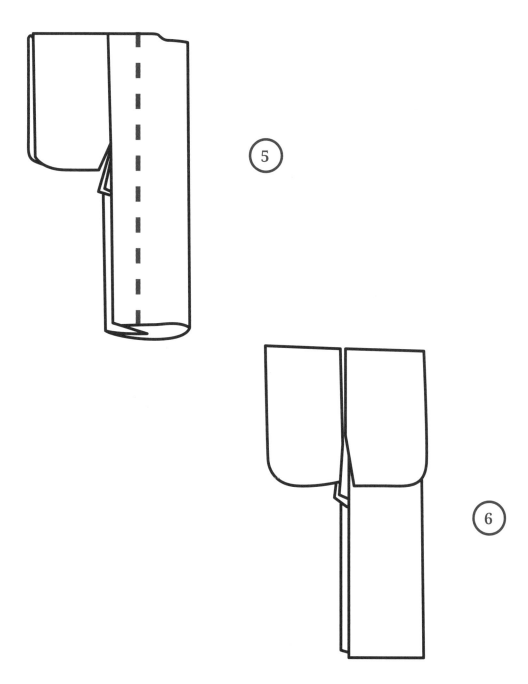

7. Fold up the bottom of the kimono so that it meets the top.

8. Flip the kimono over and fold over the remaining sleeve.

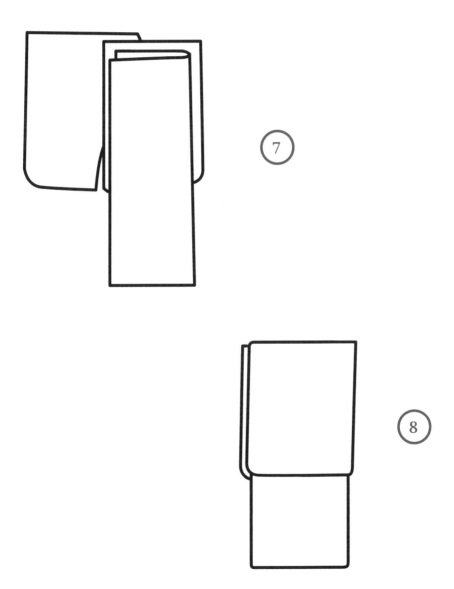

Before storing your kimono, you may want to lightly iron or steam the fabric to remove any wrinkles. To avoid burning the fabric, make sure to set your iron for the fabric your kimono is made of, and test a small area first.

Kimono are best stored in dark, dry places that cannot be accessed by animals, insects, or moisture. In Japan, you can buy special wooden cabinets and drawers called **tansu** (箪笥) that are akin to a chest of drawers in Western homes. Storing your kimono in these is optimal, but if space is tight, you can use plastic containers as long as nothing damaging to the garment can get in. Also available are Japanese paper wrappers called **tatoshi** (畳紙), which allow you to easily store and identify your kimono. These are easily found online and cost a few dollars each.

LISTING YOUR ITEM

Once the laborious prep work is complete, it is time to list your item on the online selling site of your choosing. It's wise to look up commissions and fees beforehand to ensure that your venture will be profitable. One of the biggest problems when it comes to selling kimono are the words used in the title of the item. Many people do not research what they have, or they try to use words that are familiar to English-speaking people but incredibly false, so you'll want to stay clear of any of this if you want to be an honest seller with a good reputation. Here are some helpful tips to keep in mind.

Researching Market Prices

The values given in this book are current as of the time of publication, but you should expect some variation. The best way to determine a price is to search for completed (i.e., sold) online listings of kimono. Be as specific as possible and use the proper terms.

Words That You Should Never Use in Your Listings or Descriptions

Asian

Authentic (Your item should speak for itself, and you should not have to try to validate that it is indeed a kimono of Japanese origin.)

Boho or Bohemian

Chinese

Ethnic

Feather duster

Geisha (unless you are 100 percent certain that the item that you are selling was previously owned by a real geisha and have proof)

Nightgown

Oriental

Rare

Robe

Samurai

Sizes (Kimono are a one-size-fits-all item, so any attempt at sizing is unnecessary.)

Traditional (Technically all kimono and related items are traditional to Japan, so this is redundant.)

Wrap

Details That You Should Always Include in Your Listings or Descriptions

Type of kimono or type of article or type of obi

Period in which the item was made

Material

Main motifs

Proper age classification: vintage or antique

Color

Resources

Whether looking for more information on collecting or wearing kimono, these sources will help you learn more about the world of this unique form of Japanese dress.

BOOKS

The Book of Kimono by Norio Yamanaka
This book is the best source for starter knowledge on how to wear kimono and how to store them properly. It has been reprinted many times since its original English publication in the 1980s, and the text is just as informative today as it was back then.

Kimono by Liza Dalby
One of the foremost researchers of Japanese kimono culture, with a specialty in geisha, Dalby gives a great background on the history of kimono, their development, and many other insightful facts.

Okimono Kimono by Mokona of CLAMP
An excellent book showing how a high-profile professional artist has come to include kimono in her everyday life. Includes gorgeous original designs, interviews, and coordination tips.

WEBSITES

Sou Japan | www.net-qp.com
The largest online kimono store, with prices to match any budget

The Internet Kimono Archive | www.kimono-archive.com
An online database featuring images from kimono owners around the world

Ohio Kimono | www.ohiokimono.com
A highly reputable dealer located in Ohio that takes their time to find the right fit for their customers. Their stock comes from a multigenerational, family-owned business in Kyoto.

Kurokami Kanzashi | www.etsy.com/shop/KurokamiKanzashi
A long-standing dealer of kimono and other Japanese goods, located in Canada

Glossary

A

aizome (藍染): "Indigo dye," a natural dye made from the leaves of the indigo plant. During the Edo period, it was restricted to use by only the lowest classes, such as farmers and laborers.

andon bakama (行灯袴): "Lantern pants," the undivided type of hakama.

arashi (嵐): "Storm," a type of shibori dyeing that begins by placing the fabric around a pole, which is then tied off and submerged into a vat of dye.

asa (麻): A natural plant fiber that was widely used prior to the introduction of synthetic materials. It is not as strong as silk, so finding items made from hemp tends to be rare. In English it is known as hemp.

awase (袷): "Lined kimono," a kimono with an inner lining that does not have the outer material showing through. Many older kimono did have the outer pattern continue onto the lining of their kimono, for a 360° effect.

B

benibana (紅花): "Crimson flower," a type of dye made from the stamens of saffron flowers.

bingata (紅型): "Red stencil," a type of stencil resist dye method pioneered in Okinawa. Its name comes from the traditional mulberry leaf paper that is used to create the stencils.

C

chirimen (ちりめん): A type of silk crepe that is on the heavier side and keeps the wearer warm in cold weather.

chūfurisode (中振袖): "Middle furisode," a furisode with 100-centimeter-long (39 inch) sleeves. It can be used for both formal and informal kimono.

chuya obi (典雅帯): "Night-and-day obi," an obi with different designs on each side.

cotton: *See* wata.

D

darari obi (だらりの帯): "Dangling obi," an extremely long obi worn by maiko. It is marked with a kamon on the end.

date eri (伊達衿): "Showing-off eri," a special type of eri that is sewn onto the lining of a kimono instead of a juban. It is made to give the illusion that a person is wearing more kimono than they really are.

datejime (伊達締め): "Showing-off tie," a tie that goes over the kimono to cover the koshihimo and provide a place for the obi to be tied.

dochugi (道中着): "Along-the-way wear," a jacket much like a haori except that one side folds over the other to completely cover the kimono underneath.

domawari (胴回り): "Measurement around the waist," the part of an obi that will be seen at the front of a person when worn.

donuki (胴抜): "Undergarment (to be worn in layers)," a second kimono that is decorated to look like an additional kimono along the edges where it will be seen sticking out from the main kimono, but is primarily made up of cheaper, often juban-style fabrics to save on cost.

E

Edo komon (江戸小紋): "Edo-style komon," a komon with such small and intricately stenciled patterns that it looks like an iromuji.

eri (襟/衿): "Collar," the part of a juban that is usually white and allows for other pieces of cloth to be sewn onto it to create a more decorative look and feel.

eri shin (衿芯): "Eri core," a stiff piece of board that is inserted under the eri to keep it in place when worn.

F

fukuro obi (袋帯): "Sack obi," a type of obi where only 60 percent is covered in motifs to save on cost. The non patterned parts are not seen when worn.

furisode (振袖): "Swinging sleeves," a kimono with long sleeves that almost touch the ground. They are worn by unmarried women and get their name by the fluttering that the sleeves are supposed to attract a potential suitor.

G

geisha (芸者): "Person of art / artist," a woman who had devoted her life to the pursuit of various traditional Japanese art forms such as dance, musical instruments, tea ceremony, flower arranging, and more. In the southern parts of the country, they are often referred to as **geiko** (芸妓), which means "woman of art."

H

haba (幅): "Width," the width of a panel of kimono fabric.

hadajuban (肌襦袢): "(Close to) skin underwear," a T-shirt-like, form-fitting garment worn underneath a juban to prevent it from getting stained by perspiration.

hagoromo (羽衣): "Feather robe," a transparent furisode worn on top of an outfit the give the wearer an ethereal look. The term comes from the story of the Hagoromo, a feather robe that allowed the gods to fly.

hakama (袴): "Divided skirt"; the equivalent of pants, they are worn to allow the user to have more freedom of movement without showing any skin below the waist.

hakkake (八掛): "Hanging cloth," the inner lining of the kimono hem.

hanhaba obi (半幅帯): "Half-width obi," an obi with approximately half the width of a full-size obi and used mostly for informal outfits.

hanjuban (半襦袢): "Half underwear," the top half of a two-piece juban that consists of the collar and sleeve pieces.

hanten (半纏): "Half wrap," a jacket very similar to a happi but padded. This makes it useful for winter wear.

haori (羽織): "Woven feathers," a type of jacket worn over kimono. It is held closed in the front by special ties known as "haori himo."

haori himo (羽織紐): "Haori ties," a pair of ties that hold a haori together. They are attached to small loops inside the collar of the haori and are knotted in the front. In formal situations, a string of jade or coral beads is used.

happi (法被): "Working coat," a type of jacket with form-fitting sleeves that was once worn during everyday, laborious work but is now used at outdoor festivals in the summer.

Heisei period (平成時代): Lasting from 1989 to 2019, it is the time of the internet age and a kimono revival.

heko obi (兵児帯): "Soft obi," a half-width obi made from flexible fabric that is easy to tie.

hemp: *See* asa.

hifu (被布): "Shelter cloth," a vest worn by young children over their kimono to prevent it from getting dirty.

hikizuri (引き摺り): "Trailing garment," a type of kimono with an extra-long hem worn trailing on the floor by professional artists, such as geisha and kabuki actors, when performing traditional Japanese dance.

hitoe (単衣): "Unlined kimono," a kimono that does not have an inner lining and consists of only one layer of fabric. This is done to keep the wearer cooler in the summer or to save on cost.

hiyoku (比翼): "Extra wing," an extra hem sewn onto kimono to give the effect that the wearer is wearing more than one kimono.

houmongi (訪問着): "Visiting wear," the second-most-formal type of kimono worn by married women. It is characterized by its sweeping motifs, which create a single, connected motif along the entire garment.

I

iro (色): "Color," a blanket term that describes any color but black.

iromuji (色無地): "Single plain color," a kimono that lacks decoration and whose fabric is only a single, solid color.

itajime (板締め): "Tightening boards," a shibori technique that sees fabric folded, pleated, and tied off with string before being pressed between two boards and submerged into a vat of dye.

J

jinken (人絹): "Man-made silk," a versatile synthetic fabric made to look and feel like silk, with the added bonus of being able to be washed in a normal washing machine. Known in English as "rayon."

juban (襦袢): "Underwear," a simplistic garment worn under a kimono that is meant to give the effect of the wearer having an additional kimono on and prevent any inappropriate skin to peek out.

junihitoe (十二単): "Twelve layers," an old court outfit from the Heian period (794–1185) that consisted of twelve carefully layered kimono to match the current season.

K

kakeshita (掛下): "Hanging down," a type of kimono worn trailing on the floor by brides on their wedding day.

kaku obi (角帯): "Stiff obi," a half-width obi made from stiff fabric that is meant to give its knot a crisp, sharp edge.

kamishimo (裃): "Top and bottom parts," the full outfit consisting of kataginu and haori traditionally worn by men on formal occasions.

kamon (家紋): "Family crest," a pictorial symbol of a family or that of a clan. There are tens of thousands of different family symbols, but their use has greatly diminished on contemporary kimono.

kanoko (鹿の子): "Deer fawn," a type of shibori style that produces small, square-shaped patterns that resemble those of a young deer.

kappōgi (割烹着): "Cooking wear," a special apron that protects kimono while cooking.

karieba (仮絵羽): "Temporary haori," any type of kimono jacket that is roughly tacked together to give an idea of what the finished product will look like.

karinui (仮縫い): "Temporary stitching," any type of kimono that is roughly stitched together to show the viewer what its finished shape will look like.

kasane (襲): "Layering fabric," the art of layering fabrics over the top of one another to make a fashionable statement. During the Taisho period, it was not uncommon for parents to order a set of kimono to be worn one over the other by their daughter for her wedding.

kasuri (飛白): "Jumping white," pre-dyed threads used in the production of meisen garments.

kataginu (肩衣): "Shoulder robe," a set of shoulder coverings that attach to hakama and are worn during formal occasions.

katazome (型染): "Stencil dye," a dye-resist method developed on the main islands of Japan. It uses a stencil along with rice paste resist to create patterns on fabrics.

kimono (着物): "Thing to wear," encompasses garments made from a set of panels that are sewn together in such a fashion that they make a one-size-fits-all robe. It is the national costume of Japan and comes in many different types and styles.

kinsha (金紗): A light chirimen cloth used in summer kimono.

kinu (絹): A fabric of Asian origin made from the cocoons of silk moths. It is very strong yet light, and the most common material used in the creation of kimono. Known in English as "silk."

kitsuke (着付け): "To put on clothing," the act of putting on and wearing kimono.

kofurisode (小振袖): "Small furisode," a furisode with 85-centimeter-long (33.5 inch) sleeves. It is the least formal and is often worn with hakama.

komon (小紋): "Small pattern," an informal, everyday wear type of kimono. It is characterized by repeating patterns of small or large motifs.

korin belt (コーリンベルト): A tie used to keep the collars of the juban and kimono straight.

koshihimo (腰紐): "Waist ties," the ties that bind a kimono onto a person.

kosode (小袖): "Small sleeves," any kimono whose sleeves do not go past the wearer's waist. Most Taisho kimono had slightly longer sleeves than today, so they may go a bit beyond the waist.

kuro (黒): "Black," the most formal color for kimono.

M

maiko (舞妓): "Woman of dance," apprentice geisha who are found in southern Japan, especially in the cities of Kyoto, Nara, Nagoya, and Gifu.

maru obi (丸帯): "Circle obi," an obi that is completely patterned on both sides.

Meiji period (明治時代): Lasting from 1867 to 1912, it is the period that saw rapid growth and westernization on an unprecedented level.

meisen (銘仙): A technique that takes pre dyed threads and weaves them into intricate, often-geometric shapes.

men's kimono (男の着物): Kimono made for men. They come in solid, plain colors and lack miyatsuguchi.

michiyuki (道行): "Traveling wear," a type of jacket that has an extra panel of fabric in the front, meant to fold over and completely conceal the kimono underneath. These are often used when going out in the rain or in situations where the weather may become unpredictable.

mitsumi (三つ身): "Three-year clothing," kimono worn by small girls, most notably during shichigosan.

miyatsuguchi (身八つ口): "Person (figured) opening," the opening on the back of a sleeve.

mofuku (喪服): "Mourning wear," solid black kimono and obi worn to funerals.

musou (無双): "Matchless," a special type of haori that has unique designs on the outer fabric and inner lining that allow it to be worn with either side showing.

N

nagajuban (長襦袢): "Long underwear," a single-piece juban.

Nagoya obi (名古屋帯): "Nagoya-style obi," an obi meant to be tied in a taiko (drum) knot shape, with half being the length for the knot and half being the length for wrapping around the waist with ease.

nenneko (ねんねこ): A haori/hanten hybrid traditionally worn by mothers while carrying their babies on their backs. The term derives from a ditty sung at the beginning of traditional lullabies.

O

obi (帯): "Belt," a long sash worn around the waist that originally held the kimono in place when worn.

obiage (帯揚げ): "Obi raiser," a piece of cloth that covers the obi makura and helps keeps the obi up.

obidome (帯留め): "Obi fastener," a decoration that sits on the obijime.

obi ita (帯板): "Obi board," a flat board placed between the layers of the obi in the front of the wearer to keep the area smooth.

obijime (帯締め): "Obi tie," a cord used to keep the obi on the wearer.

obi makura (帯枕): "Obi pillow," a pillow to keep the obi upright in the back. Most frequently used with Nagoya obi.

omeshi chirimen (御召ちりめん): "Chirimen summons clothing," a luxurious type of weave that uses chirimen silk as its base.

omiyamairi (お宮参り): "Shrine visit," the first visit that a child makes to their local shrine to be blessed by a priest shortly after birth. It is akin to a Christian baptism.

oridashi (織り出し): "End of the weave," a woven line to designate the end of an obi.

ōfurisode (大振袖): "Large furisode," a furisode with 120-centimeter-long (47 inch) sleeves. These are used for the most formal furisode.

ōganji wasō (オーガンジー和装): "Organza Japanese-style clothing," another name for "Hagoromo" (*see above*).

P

polyester (ポリエステル): A synthetic fabric that is cheap to produce and washes easily.

R

rayon: *See* jinken.

Reiwa period (令和時代): The current era. It is a time of experimentation and making old things new again.

rinzu (綸子): "Figured silk," a luxurious process that involves weaving patterns and designs into the base fabric before applying the main motifs.

ro (絽): A summer silk that is woven with horizontal lines to allow for more air flow, keeping the wearer cool in the heat.

ryōzuma (両褄): "Mirror pattern," a type of design from the Early Taisho period that features almost identical patterns on each side of a kimono's hem.

S

senui (背縫い): "Back seam," the seam that runs along the middle of the back of a kimono.

sha (紗): A type of sheer, light silk used for summer kimono. It is also called "silk gauze."

shibori (絞り): "Tie-dye," a method of dyeing that requires sections of the fabric to be tied or sewn off with thread to create a resist pattern that is visible after submerging the fabric into a vat of dye.

shichigosan (七五三): "7-5-3," a special celebration where boys aged three and five and girls aged three and seven go to their local shrines to pray for health and prosperity in the future.

shioze (塩瀬): A thick, woven silk that is used most commonly in items that will endure much folding and creasing.

shiromuku (白無垢): "Pure-white dress," an all-white uchikake worn by a bride during the wedding ceremony. The color white is a symbol of purity and fresh beginnings.

Showa period (昭和時代): Lasting from 1926 to 1989, it saw the rise of nationalism, World War II, the American occupation, and a time of rapid modernization.

shusu (繻子): A satin-like silk known for its thickness and ability to hold heavy embroidery.

silk: *See* kinu.

sode (袖): "Sleeve," the sleeve of a kimono.

sodeguchi (袖口): "Sleeve mouth," the opening of a sleeve for the hand to go through.

susohiki (裾引き): "Trailing skirt," the southern dialect word for "hikizuri."

susosen (裾先): "Hemline," the bottom hem of a kimono.

susoyoke (裾除け): "Removable skirt," the bottom half of a two-piece juban that encompasses the hem from the waist down.

T

Taisho period (大正時代): Lasting from 1912 to 1926, it was the renaissance of kimono production.

tansu (箪笥): "Chest of drawers," a large set of drawers made specifically for storing kimono and obi.

taresaki (たれ先): "Before the hanging end," the end of an obi marked with the oridashi. It will almost always hang down from an obi's knot.

tatoshi (畳紙): "Folding paper," special paper wrappers used for storing kimono and obi.

tesaki (手先): "Fingers," the beginning of an obi that will be held by a person while they tie the rest of the obi.

tomesode (留袖): "Fastened sleeves," the most formal type of kimono worn by a married woman. It gets its name from furisode sleeves, which were traditionally cut once a woman married. A tomesode will never have any sort of decoration above the waist.

tsujigahana (辻が花): "Trailing flowers," an old technique revived by Itchiku Kubota in the 1980s. It is a very labor-intensive process that involves hand painting, tie-dyeing, and weaving.

tsuke obi (付け帯): "Fixed obi," a type of obi that has been modified for easy wearing.

tsukesage (付下げ): "Attached downward," the midlevel of kimono formality. It gets its name from motifs that stay only within their own panel and do not connect across the garment like that of a houmongi and always point up toward the shoulders.

tsume tsuzure (爪綴れ): "Nail weaving," a labor-intensive process of weaving that uses one's fingernails to create intricately woven motifs on a loom.

tsumugi (紬): "Pongee," a weaving technique that involves knotting.

tsutsugaki (筒型): "Tube mold," a cheaper version of yuzen dyeing that uses small tubes of sticky rice paste as a resist for dyeing and decorating fabrics. It was almost always used in conjunction with indigo dye.

U

uchikake (打掛): "Dragging outer garment," a formal type of kimono originally worn by nobility that is now worn by brides on their wedding day. It is characterized by its heavily padded hem and elaborate designs.

umamori (馬乗り): "Horse-riding pants," the divided style of hakama.

urushi (漆): "Lacquer," a liquid shellac that threads are dipped in before being woven into garments. It gives the finished piece a shine that can be seen from far away.

W

wafuku (和服): "Native dress," a term encompassing all styles of clothing that originated in Japan. Kimono is a type of wafuku.

wata (綿): A lightweight plant fiber used in the making of informal kimono items such as yukata. Known in English as "cotton."

wool: *See* yomo.

Y

yomo (羊毛): "Sheep's hair," fabrics made from the hair of sheep. They tend to be used for informal kimono items or winter items, since wool insulates the wearer but does not have the shine or softness that silk does. Known in English as "wool."

yukata (浴衣): "Bathrobe," the most informal type of kimono. They are made from light fabrics such as cotton and are worn only during the summer months to keep cool.

Yuki tsumugi (結城紬): A special type of tsumugi that originated in the Yuki area. It is an Important Intangible Cultural Properties of Japan and is also on the UNESCO Representative List of the Intangible Cultural Heritage of Humanity list.

yuzen (友禅): A labor-intensive method of applying dye-resist paste, painting in desired sections, washing, and repeating for different colors.

Acknowledgments

This book would not have existed were it not for my parents, Marianne and Milan. I grew up surrounded by their love of all things Japanese and came to admire the many antiques that practically littered our house when I was a child. Thank you for exposing me to this unique environment and for allowing me to pursue my passions, even though it may have driven you crazy at times.

My writing skills would not be where they are now without the help of Tsuneko Iwai, my Japanese language teacher. She opened up an entirely new understanding of Japanese to me and has never failed to answer my many questions over the years. Thank you for teaching me the basics of this wonderful language and for allowing me to bridge the gap between English and Japanese in a way that both sides can understand.

My knowledge and collection directly stem from Christina Stoppa, who has been my closest kimono friend and advisor for over ten years. I think I've learned more from you than anyone else. Thank you for being on this amazing journey with me, especially for always helping me correctly identify what I've found from lackluster sellers' photographs and to provide an excellent source of discussion in the middle of the night.

A special thanks is due to all of my online supporters who were enthusiastic about the project from the beginning and eagerly anticipated any update that I had to give.

Index

Other Schiffer Books on Related Subjects:

 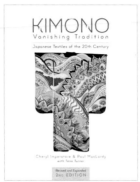 

Traditional Kimono Silks, Anita Yasuda, 978-0-7643-2691-2

Kimono, Vanishing Tradition: Japanese Textiles of the 20th Century, 2nd edition,
Cheryl Imperatore and Paul MacLardy with Tena Turner, 978-0-7643-5050-4

Japan, Hans Sautter, 978-0-7643-6498-3

Library of Congress Control Number: 2023941132

Cover and interior design by Danielle D. Farmer
Type set in Droid Serif/Minion Pro/Ainslie Sans

ISBN: 978-0-7643-6586-7
Printed in China

Published by Schiffer Publishing, Ltd.
4880 Lower Valley Road
Atglen, PA 19310
Phone: (610) 593-1777; Fax: (610) 593-2002
Email: info@schifferbooks.com
Web: www.schifferbooks.com

For our complete selection of fine books on this and related subjects, please visit our website at www.schifferbooks.com. You may also write for a free catalog.

Schiffer Publishing's titles are available at special discounts for bulk purchases for sales promotions or premiums. Special editions, including personalized covers, corporate imprints, and excerpts, can be created in large quantities for special needs. For more information, contact the publisher.